DE...
CONN...ON

TOYNE NEWTON

Toyne was born in Clapham, London SW2 in 1950. His family moved to Sussex some five years later. In 1974 he enrolled at the West Sussex College of Design studying photography and graphic design. On graduating he worked as a photographer and in Audio Visual Communications for a while before becoming a freelance feature writer for the Unexplained Magazine and subsequently an authority on the occult.

He is now a full time writer and magazine contributor.

CHARLES WALKER

Charles was born in Worthing, Sussex in 1953 and educated at a local Church of England school. He has worked as a sales assistant in various local establishments and, more recently, taught word processing and computer skills.

Charles, who is considered to be one of the countries foremost authorities on the occult and paranormal, has contributed to various magazines. He uncovered the existance of a bizarre satanic group, The Friends of Hekate' in Sussex some years ago. It was at this time he teamed up with fellow authors Toyne Newton and Alan Brown to produce 'The Demonic Connection'. Since then he, together with his wife Jean, has spent a great deal of time tracing their activities, and occult practises in general, throughout the country.

Charles is now a full time researcher and writer on occult matters.

ALAN BROWN

Alan Was born in 1956 and is a native of Southampton. He is a graduate of Southampton University and has contributed short stories and articles to various magazines. He is now a novelist with several books to his credit.

THE DEMONIC CONNECTION

An Investigation into Satanism in
England and the International
Black Magic Conspiracy

TOYNE NEWTON

CHARLES WALKER

& ALAN BROWN

Badgers Books

Published in Great Britain by
Badgers Books, 8–10 Gratwicke Road, Worthing,
Sussex. BN11 4BH.
1993.

First published by Blandford Press 1987.

A catalogue record for this book is available
from the British Library.

ISBN   1 898230 00 5

Printed and bound in the U.K. by
Cox & Wyman Ltd.,
Reading, Berkshire.

CONTENTS

ACKNOWLEDGEMENTS

My grateful thanks are due to my Mother for her patient help,
my two colleagues for their painstaking research and determination, Mary and Elymas for their invaluable counsel,
Biologist Dr Andrew Allen, Mr R. Harmer, the Local Studies
Librarian at Chichester, Staff of the Goring and Worthing
Libraries, and to my friends for their helpful advice, including in
particular, John Tobler for his support and vision.

                                                              T.N.

FOREWORD

by the Reverend Canon Dominic Walker, OGS

A knock on the vicarage door can be full of surprises. It may be a routine enquiry about baptism, marriage or funeral arrangements; it may be a tramp in need of a sandwich and a cup of tea or someone wanting to hire the church hall or borrow the church keys; it may be someone with a personal problem or in deep distress. All require immediate attention although some are easier to deal with than others.

I can recall opening the door to be met with, 'Father, we've got a ghost, please come quickly,' or 'I think I'm possessed by the Devil, you've got to help me.' Then there have been the groups of youngsters looking anxious and quickly electing a spokesman to announce, 'You see, Vicar, we thought it was just a bit of fun and then the glass started to move and it scared the hell out of us.'

The most alarming cases, however, have been where the enquirer has made an appointment, walked uneasily into the house, quickly looked away from the crucifix on the wall and begun with, 'I don't know where to turn or who to trust. I've got involved in an occult group and now I can't get out.' The tale has a familiar ring. Invited along to meet a few friends or to have a bit of fun for those interested in the occult, the initiate finds he has joined something he knows little about. Perhaps lured by the sexual side of the group, the initiate soon finds that he has been compromised and can't get out. His life is no longer his own and he must either stay in or take the risk of making the break.

The word 'occult' means 'hidden', referring not only to the

'hidden' mysteries to which the occultists claim to have access, but often to the groups and individuals who are involved in the black arts or in Satanism. In the well-publicised 1986 'Satanist trial' at Maidstone, in his summing up Judge Neil Denison said to the jury: 'I suggest that you approach your assessment of the evidence against the background that Satanism does exist, and there can be no doubt that those that practise it are evil, depraved, and dangerous.'

The occult has an alluring fascination for many youngsters who are often disenchanted with the Christian church, or with life in general. The rise in the number of cults is also disturbing and indicates a need for unquestioning belief in something, the need to belong and the need to follow a powerful leader no matter how unorthodox or demanding. The real world, where life is uncertain, and where the church questions beliefs and traditions cannot provide an attractive home for insecure youngsters or for those who want their lives lived for them.

Toyne Newton and his researchers began their journey by investigating a local Sussex 'legend' and stumbled on something. Their curiosity aroused, their journey led them into a world of recent tales and ancient beliefs, and even into the occult beliefs behind Hitler, present day politics and the possibility of parapsychology as a weapon in warfare.

Whilst the Christian church seeks to help the casualties of the occult and those who are spiritually, psychically and psychologically disturbed and the theologians look at the nature of evil and the existence or non-existence of the Devil (who incidentally is never mentioned in the Christian Creeds), investigators like Toyne Newton and his team keep before us the reality of evil.

Dominic Walker, OGS
Brighton, 1986

BRAMBER RAPE

The section of land known as the Rape of Bramber stretches centrally from east to west of the English county of Sussex and from the coast northwards to the Surrey border, its most prominent feature being the range of chalky South Downs which rise to nearly 800 feet in places. It contains the rivers Adur and Arun and there is much evidence for prehistoric and Roman settlement in the southern part of the rape, which was also thickly settled in the Saxon and Medieval periods.

Of the four towns of the rape, Steyning (of Saxon origin and formerly a port on the Adur) became superseded in this function by New Shoreham in the late eleventh century, at which time castled Bramber was also a 'new town'.

Horsham grew in importance in the later Middle Ages, becoming one of the chief towns of the rape in the seventeenth and eighteenth centuries, whilst the fourth town, Worthing, began only as a resort *circa* 1800, but expanded so fast in the twentieth century that by 1978 building along the coastline was almost continuous, leaving land in the rest of the rape largely rural.

Whilst there may have been divisions of the county called rapes in Saxon times, it seems the Sussex rapes originated after the Norman Conquest.

William de Braose, who held in demesne a number of manors in a triangular area between Clapham in the west, Southwick in the east, and Shipley in the north, was granted the Bramber rape in 1073, and it is in the Clapham area of this triangle that our investigations are mostly concentrated.

INTRODUCTION

One evening in the mid-autumn of 1978, Charles Walker, who was investigating various mysterious happenings in Clapham Wood on the South Downs, received an intriguing telephone call from a well-spoken man who declined to identify himself but who claimed to have knowledge of the strange incidents currently being reported in the Press.

His curiosity roused, Charles agreed to meet the unknown man that evening at a crossways in the privately-owned woods where several public pathways intersect amongst woodland dense with sweet chestnut trees, from which the area takes its name.

It was dark when he arrived at the rendezvous, access to which is via a kissing-gate off the busy A 27 dual carriageway, and as he walked into the quiet, brooding wood he couldn't help wondering if he'd been wise in keeping the appointment. For this was the area where distressed dog-owners had reported their pets had suddenly disappeared without trace, whilst others had maintained that their dogs had suffered sudden inexplicable epileptic fits and had had to be destroyed, and where even people had been overcome by powerful unseen forces. Anything could happen, Charles thought, and he was completely alone.

But even as prickles of fear chilled his spine and he was contemplating a hasty retreat to the safety of the highway, a man's voice boomed out from the clump of bushes he was passing: 'Don't attempt to look for me! For your safety and mine it is imperative you do not see who I am!'

Recognising the warning voice as that of his telephone caller, Charles stopped dead in his tracks. He did not attempt to look around: indeed, the whole conversation that followed was carried on over his shoulder as the ominous, cultured voice addressed him from somewhere within the dense shrubs.

The man claimed to be an initiate of a secret group formed in Sussex. 'The nearest I can describe our activities to you is that we are followers of Satanism,' he told Charles. 'At every meeting we hold we sacrifice some animal or other, usually a dog or other domestic or farm animal depending on what's available at the time,' and as the impassive voice chronicled the vile practices of the cult, Charles felt his blood run cold.

What was happening in these woods? Who were these evil people? Why were they causing so much suffering and distress?

The initiate's response to his troubled questions was merely to deliver a stern warning not to interfere in their activities because they intended to continue using Clapham Wood where conditions were ideal for their purposes. He spoke of people in high places holding positions of power who were directly involved and who would brook no interference, and ended warningly: 'We will stop at nothing to ensure the safety of our cult.'

As Charles regained the nearby A 27 with its bright lights and constant flow of traffic, he felt he was stepping back from another world – from the dark world of medieval Britain with all its magic, murder and mayhem. Who would believe his story in this England of 1978? Even he, a practical down-to-earth person, was finding difficulty in accepting the reality of the bizarre meeting.

Yet the sense of foreboding which hung like a pall over the area was real enough, for too many people had reported experiencing strange feelings here, some saying they felt intense pains in the body, pressure in the head, sickness and dizziness, while yet others had become suddenly weak and lost their balance. Several mystified dog-owners had reported the sudden and complete disappearance of their unfortunate dogs whilst others complained of temporary paralysis and dementia over-coming their pets. Here, too, there had been many reports of Unidentified Flying Objects and strange lights in the sky, and the whole area was steeped in mystery. What did it all mean?

Despite the initiate's warning, Charles was determined to find out. Besides, there was another, more disturbing reason why he should not allow himself to be put off, because a short time previously – on All Hallows Eve – the Reverend Harry Neil Snelling, retired Vicar of Clapham, had gone missing. Extensive searches by police and local people who knew the woods well had not revealed his whereabouts, and in view of what Charles had just been told he had a grim gut feeling about the fate of the kindly old cleric. Now, more than ever, his lonely investigations must go on ...

It was shortly after this period that I myself began researching into the enigma of Clapham Wood, and later had an article on the subject published in the London-based magazine *The Unexplained* which provoked quite a lot of correspondence. In fact it was through this that Charles and I, and latterly Alan Brown (to whom I am indebted for the use of some material from his original manuscript) came together and decided on a joint investigation into the baffling series of incidents which, although we didn't realise it at the time, proved to be only the tip of the iceberg.

As we progressed and delved deeper into history, we found link after link leading us inexorably on – from history to legend, from legend to myth, from myth to magic and from magic back to grim reality – the whole culminating in a shattering realisation of the malevolence uncovered, which extends nationally and, perhaps, beyond.

What is this latent occult force that can be tapped, harnessed and so manipulated that it can harm physically as well as mentally, humans as well as animals? Who are these intellectual transgressors – these faceless ones, protected as they are by the hierarchy of their secret cults – who are using this power so indiscriminately for their own ends and who are practising here in our country, in the very heart of our villages, now? What are their ultimate aims?

Perhaps our fate as a nation lies not so much in the threat of nuclear war as in the answer to this vital question.

Toyne Newton
Goring-by-Sea, 1986

1 REPORTED PHENOMENA

'The truth is that once a human being strays out of the world of the commonplace and is invited to contemplate the extravagant, he becomes numbed. The next time he encounters the abnormal he cannot register it; he says ..."Such things don't happen".'

Rebecca West
Introduction to Hugh Thomas's *The Murder of Rudolph Hess*

DISAPPEARING DOGS

'Man's best friend', the dog, has always held a very special place in the households and hearts of pet lovers in this country, so when in 1975 the Worthing Press carried reports of sudden disappearances and mysterious symptoms and illness amongst dogs being exercised in a certain part of Clapham Wood, many pet owners came forward, not only to express their alarm but also to recount their own strange experiences of the area.

'Wallace', a three-year-old chow belonging to Mr and Mrs Peter Love of Patching, was being taken for a walk by their son to the popular wooded area known as The Chestnuts, when it 'just disappeared'. It was a wintry April in 1975 with a cold northerly wind inhibiting new growth, so cover was sparse. The chow ran in amongst some bare trees and failed to reappear despite being constantly called. A thorough search was instigated, but no trace of the dog was ever found.

A week later, a two-year-old collie belonging to Mr John Cornford, a Clapham farmer, also disappeared without trace at practically the same spot. It was last seen going off towards the trees and, normally obedient, failed to respond to repeated calls. Mr Cornford organised a search but the unfortunate dog was never found.

A golden retriever belonging to Mr E.F. Rawlins of Worthing

became partially paralysed after running in the woods and later had to be destroyed, whilst a collie owned by Mrs E.T. Wells of Durrington became so agitated on nearing this area of the woods that, happily for the dog's well-being, she immediately took it back home.

Fortunately, also, the owner of a pug did likewise when, on approaching the trees where the other dogs had disappeared, her dog began shaking so violently and foaming at the mouth, its eyes bulging as if in an epileptic fit, that she snatched it up and rushed back to her car parked nearby. The dog soon regained its equilibrium and the veterinary surgeon whom she consulted as soon as she arrived home could find no physical reason for the dog's strange behaviour, and pronounced it fit. Other owners, however, have reported their dogs as being similarly smitten by sudden frightening attacks of epilepsy, and recovering once they left the area.

Commenting to a reporter, Mrs J. Strickland, a dog breeder in Clapham village, said that she didn't exercise her dogs there because the woods were full of pheasants, but the fact of the disappearing dogs was genuine and no satisfactory explanation had ever been given.

When it was suggested that a shoot may have been in progress at the time and the dogs accidentally shot, all the owners of the missing animals were adamant about one thing: they had heard no shots, no warning shouts, no cries of distress or other evidence whatsoever; their pets had just 'disappeared into thin air', silently, in the quietness of the woods, in the presence of no other human beings save their owners.

On one occasion, a horse disappeared when its rider left it tethered to a tree while he relieved himself in the woods, returning moments later to find the animal gone. It was never seen again.

HUMAN REACTIONS

In addition to its effect on animals, people have also claimed to have experienced a variety of strange feelings in this particular part of Clapham Wood.

Mrs Goodman of Findon reported that while she was taking her dog for a walk near the woods (she didn't actually go into them as she had read about the strange happenings there so began walking in the opposite direction) she experienced great difficulty in getting away from the wood. 'It was as though I was being pulled back, and my legs grew weak,' she said. Her dog, also, seemed to be experiencing difficulty, but they 'battled and struggled on', and when they came to a certain spot, suddenly 'I was free', Mrs Goodman commented, adding, 'It was quite frightening. There is something strange about that wood.'

Several people have claimed to have felt themselves being literally pushed over by an invisible force while walking in The Chestnuts area, whilst others have come over faint, or felt their limbs jerking uncontrollably.

One man felt as if his eardrums were being 'pulled inside out', and many have spoken of feeling unusual pressure in their heads, but all confirm that as soon as they were away from the immediate area (about 50 yards farther on) their symptoms disappeared as mysteriously as they had come.

Those walking together were affected simultaneously, although their actual symptoms were different: headaches, dizziness, stomach cramps, sudden weakness in the limbs, shakiness and, in some cases, disturbing feelings of being pulled by an unseen force, the range of complaints obviously depending on the susceptibility of the individual concerned.

Some people have even reported that while driving along the nearby A 27 past this particular area of woodland, they have felt their steering wheels being pulled round in the direction of the woods as if suddenly magnetised. Two of the people who experienced this phenomenon – Mr Ison, a down-to-earth builder, and Mrs Peters, a practical nursing sister – each made similar comments in that they were almost overwhelmed by a desire to 'let the steering-wheel have its own way', which, on a dual carriageway, could have had disastrous results. As with Mrs Goodman, however, they managed to fight and overcome the alarming influence until safely out of range.

MISTY GREY SHAPES

There have been two reports of 'localised mist appearing from nowhere' along the public footpaths in this area. On a perfectly clear summer evening, two hikers traversing The Chestnuts saw a sudden puff of mist writhing before them and forming itself into a bear-like shape, whilst on another occasion, also on a clear evening, a party of three walking together in the same area simultaneously experienced a drop in temperature, which became normal as they hurriedly progressed along the footpath. On looking back, however, they saw a grey mist patch collecting on the pathway and rapidly begin forming into quite a solid shape, the top part of which was recognisable even in the descending dusk, as the pointed, fox-like head of an animal. Taking fright, they ran from the scene. All the hikers said they felt very uneasy in the spooky atmosphere, so none of them lingered to investigate further, but all were sure they had witnessed the beginnings of a manifestation of some kind.

LACK OF WILDLIFE

Visitors to Clapham Wood, especially in the area under discussion, have constantly remarked on the lack of wildlife and birds, birdsong seeming to be almost non-existent. Whereas Mr David Bennett, churchwarden of Clapham church, used to record the song of the nightingale in these woods in the early 1970s, by the end of the decade the presence of this Downland songster had completely disappeared.

Mr George Juggins, woodman in Clapham Wood, said that during his long association with the place many birds had been lost, and although the woods used to be yellow with primroses, nowadays (he was speaking in 1983) there were practically none.

Rabbits, squirrels, badgers and foxes still occasionally put in an appearance, he said, though nothing like as often as they used to, and according to another resident, an uncanny silence descends upon the whole wood at certain times, for which no-one has ever given an adequate explanation.

Of the sparsity of wildlife and the rather oppressive atmosphere which the dank, lifeless wood with its smell of sulphur and stagnating undergrowth seems to engender, one visitor said, 'It is as if something repellent is keeping all natural life away.'

But if the area seems deficient in its share of natural flora and fauna, there has been no shortage of reports of the supernatural: in particular, the sighting of unidentified flying objects.

UFO SIGHTINGS

During the past ten years, reports of sightings seem to have arrived in spates, and include lights of various intensity and colour, from bright white and yellow through to orange and 'glowing', appearing in an assortment of shapes from disc-like and round to ball-shaped, cigar-shaped, boomerang-shaped, oblong and the more usual saucer-shaped.

Some have been reported seen hovering over Clapham Wood, others rotating or spinning with flashing lights, and most are seen for just a few seconds before disappearing rapidly into the night sky – usually in the direction of the nearby coast. Descending and ascending beams of light have also been reported, dropping down into and zooming up from the dark woods.

The following sightings during the four years from 1979 to 1982 seem fairly representative of those recorded.

In May 1979, Leigh Chandler, a trainee nurse at Southlands Hospital, Shoreham, was travelling along the A 259 approaching Clapham at about 2.30 am when she suddenly saw an object 'glowing orange and shaped like a football cut in half' moving rapidly above the treetops from the direction of the woods across the road southwards. As the object was so close she found the experience very frightening, she said.

During the same year, Mr Barber of Findon was standing on Highdown Hill (which overlooks Clapham Wood) when he saw a large orange ball-shaped object manoeuvring above the part of the woods near the church. (There is a round pit in a clearing of the woods here, just north-west of the church, where nothing grows and no-one seems to know its origin.) Suddenly it dropped vertically, and he saw it glowing among the trees. According to the Police, this sighting was witnessed by several others who telephoned them at the time.

Mrs Moore of Littlehampton, a telephonist, was driving home after visiting friends, via Findon along the A 280 known as Long Furlong – a narrow, hilly road that winds between the Downs and open farmland – at about 1 am when she saw a 'bright circular light, larger than an aeroplane, too low and bright for a star, stationary in the sky above Clapham Woods'. All the time she was driving along the deserted road the object was visible, but as she approached Clapham she could no longer see it, and realised she would probably be passing beneath it.

'I felt immediately that it was not a natural thing and I was scared and just kept on driving,' she said. She saw the object on four separate occasions – always in the same position – between November 1980 and March 1981, and having lived in Richmond near an airport for many years, was quite sure that it was not an aircraft. Mrs Moore added that she was not the slightest bit afraid of the thought of the paranormal and readily accepted the existence of UFOs and Extra Terrestrials, 'But this was different,' she said, 'and I had an instinctive feeling that the thing could have been evil.'

On the 23 October 1981, Mr Derek Stenning of Worthing was driving home from nearby Patching at 7.30 pm when his son who was with him spotted 'a large coloured disc hovering above a clump of trees on the north of the A 27 above Clapham'. Simon, a Durrington High School pupil at the time, said that one half of the disc was red and the other white, and the two colours kept flashing alternately. Even as he pointed out the object to his father, it rose suddenly higher in the air and 'seemed to come towards the car' as it crossed the A 27 going southwards, and accelerated out to sea 'at an incredible speed'. Although the experience lasted only a matter of seconds, it left Simon feeling terrified, and even his father admitted that it 'put the fear of God' into him and was unlike anything he had ever seen.

On a clear cold February night in 1982, Jenni Sessions was driving along a coastal road in Angmering-on-Sea when she saw a large circular white light moving from the direction of Clapham towards the sea. She stopped her car, switched off the engine, and got out to watch it. It made no noise as it hovered, pulsating, over the coast. It was too large, and silent, for an aeroplane, and it suddenly sped upwards and disappeared.

In all cases where the police were informed, the Ministry of Defence were said to be investigating further, but as most UFO sightings seem to be one-to-one affairs, the scepticism of officialdom and the general public remains pretty well constant. Perhaps it was because there had been no reports of sightings over Clapham for two or three years that in the summer of 1985 some person or persons unknown decided to invent one, although, as the following report suggests, they went to an enormous amount of trouble to do so.

MYSTERIOUS CIRCLES

On Saturday, 29 June 1985, a mysterious group of five circles appeared in a wheatfield in Patching some 200 yards from the road (the A 280, Long Furlong) from which they were clearly visible. The central and largest circle was about 50 feet in diameter and was surrounded by four equidistant smaller circles each about 15 feet across. The waist-high crop had been flattened in a swirling, clockwise direction, giving the appearance of scorching, and the whole cluster gave the impression that a UFO had landed there.

The same weekend identical marks appeared, again in a wheatfield, at Bratton in Wiltshire. As at Patching, the circles were clearly visible from the road, thus providing passers-by with an uninterrupted view of the pseudo space visitor and giving much cause for speculation.

During the weekend following, i.e. 6 – 7 July, a further set of circles appeared in a wheatfield in Winchester. In this instance the Ministry of Defence said they were carrying out their own investigations as similar phenomena had been reported in the area over a number of years.

A month later, on 6 August, Southern Television reported on their *Coast-to-Coast* news programme that yet another group of five circles had been discovered, this time in Andover, Hampshire.

The dimensions of the groups of circles were the same in each case and, with the exception of those at Andover, all within sight of a busy road, as if calculated to attract maximum attention and news coverage. The Press described it as an elaborate hoax.

SPASMODIC FIRES

What cannot be regarded as a hoax concerns the number of fires in the Clapham area. On Friday, 17 November 1978, £20,000 worth of damage was caused to two farms at Clapham, and an old people's home threatened. At Long Furlong Farm, Clapham, run by the brothers Malcolm and Brian Jenkin of Myrtle Grove Farm, Patching, a barn and 3,500 bales of straw were destroyed costing £6,000, and within twenty minutes of this occurrence, Clapham Farm barns and outbuildings containing 11,500 bales of straw worth £15,000 were set alight. Altogether 11 fire appliances and 75 firemen were called to the fires, which brought the total number of fires reported in the area to 9 during the Autumn of 1978, and because of insufficient pressure in the mains, water had to be pumped from a farm well.

Although detectives were convinced the large fires were the work of an arsonist, many small intermittent fires are said to start unaccountably in the Clapham Wood area and the vicinity of Long Furlong (where car drivers have often claimed their engines have become suddenly faulty, but righted themselves later, or that the car's electrical circuits have behaved erratically), and in December 1982 one driver swerved into the hedgerow when the engine of his car suddenly caught fire. Although he was apparently treated for shock and his car towed away, no-one admitted any knowledge of the incident afterwards, the Worthing Police maintaining that the Littlehampton Police would have made any necessary report of the matter, and *vice versa*, and all that was left by way of evidence next day was a small section of charred hedge.

Verification of such minor incidents is never easy to come by. Local residents as well as officials can be adept at the art of fobbing off both the vulgarly curious and the seeker after the truth. Such reticence is understandable from the point of view of unwarranted invasion of privacy or damage to property such as that which occurred in the July 1985 UFO hoax when Mr Wicks, manager at Tolmare Farm where the hoax previously referred to was perpetrated, was forced to mount guard on the Long Furlong road to stop sight-seers tramping through his wheatfield and doing further damage to the crop.

But where there seems no logical explanation for the type of phenomena reported in this chapter, too many people blithely say (as in our opening quotation), 'Such things don't happen.' But they do, as Charles Walker realised only too well when he was unexpectedly called to a clandestine meeting one night in Clapham Wood.

2 THE SECRET MEETING AND ITS AFTERMATH

'The smallest atom of truth represents some man's bitter toil and agony.'

H.L. Mencken

THE INITIATE'S WARNING

For several years before the disappearance of the dogs in Clapham Wood, the local *Worthing Press* had, at various times, carried reports by Clapham residents of unexplained happenings and UFO sightings in the area, and Charles Walker, a Worthing sales assistant, had been making his own investigations into the matter.

Although a support member of several groups formed locally for the study of psychic phenomena and UFO sightings, Charles, a dedicated researcher and seeker after the truth, was certainly not averse to either working or following up any lead, on his own; he had in fact been making some discreet inquiries through his personal contacts in Brighton as to whether Clapham Wood was being used by an occult group.

He had also written letters requesting anyone who had any information to contact him, and these letters, giving Charles's telephone number, were published in local newspapers.

In November 1978, it seemed that his enterprise was paying off when he received a telephone call one evening from a well-spoken man who declined to give his name, but stated quite categorically that if Charles was still interested in what was going on in Clapham Wood, that they should meet.

'Your place or mine?' Charles asked somewhat facetiously, bearing in mind the number of crank calls he'd already received, but there was no hint of amusement in the man's voice as he replied tersely, 'Neither. In Clapham Wood. At the crossroads in The Chestnuts ... in half an hour,' and promptly rang off.

As previously mentioned, this area – the scene of so many reported phenomena – was well-known to Charles, but as it was then half-past eight and the meeting was scheduled for nine o'clock, it didn't give him much time to reflect.

Who was this unknown man? Was the call genuine? Charles couldn't begin to hazard a guess, but there was something about the man's cultured voice, brusque though his manner had been, that conveyed such an air of mystery and intrigue that Charles felt at all costs he had to go along and find out.

Besides, in his innermost heart had he not been hoping for such a call? Over the past three years at least, scant information had been forthcoming ever since the media had become interested, which had had a clamming-up effect all round, and all he wanted was a lead to help him find out the truth. Here at last, dubious though the circumstances surrounding the unknown telephone caller might be, was an opportunity for him to do just that. He dare not miss it. His mind made up, Charles hastened to keep the clandestine appointment.

It was pitch dark when he arrived at the top of Titnore Hill and crossed over the dual carriageway, the A 27, on the north side of which Clapham Wood lies. Although woodland borders this road, the gateway leading to the public footpath through the woods is slightly indented, leaving space for several cars to safely park off the busy carriageway. Tonight the parking-space was empty, Charles noted, as he pushed open the small wooden kissing-gate to the right of the farm gate, negotiated some overgrown brambles, and squeezed through the narrow aperture into the black woods beyond.

His boots crunched hollowly on the hard pathway, which was overhung with foliage and sloped gently upwards, and as he progressed along it he couldn't help wondering if, after all, he'd been wise to come. He could be attacked and overcome by his unknown caller, or suffer the same fate as the disappearing dogs; no-one would know, for he had told no-one of his assignation.

Filled with sudden foreboding, he slowed his pace. Darkness pressed around him and he couldn't see his hand before his face. But he was well aware of a feeling of menace. Even by day the proliferation of foliage seemed hostile, the long sharply-toothed leaves of the sweet chestnut trees which abounded in the area intertwining with thorny shrubs and brambles making a forbidding border to the stoney up-hill path. In the dark the atmosphere became even more sinister.

Should he return? He was still within sound of the road, and could hear the reassuring hum of traffic. Glancing back, he could see the welcome headlights of passing cars, momentarily illuminating the gate by which he'd entered a few minutes previously and which seemed now to separate him from the world he knew as he walked into the world of the unknown. Charles hesitated only a moment longer, however, then strode resolutely on.

Soon he arrived at the crossroads where the footpaths intersected, marked, he knew (but couldn't see on this moonless night) by a rakish thin-armed signpost dwarfed by a single, tall, bare-barked pine tree whose straggly top fitted in well with the rest of the tangled woodland. This was the rendezvous. He walked a few yards farther on, then turned and retraced his steps. All was disturbingly silent.

He walked back and forth several times, but met nobody on the pathway; yet some strange sixth sense warned him he was not alone.

He felt his nerves tingling, whether from fear or anger at being brought on what was appearing to be a wild-goose chase, he didn't know, but just as he decided he'd better make tracks for home, a voice boomed out suddenly from amid some bushes he was passing: 'Don't attempt to look for me! For your safety and mine it is imperative you do not see who I am!'

Charles froze, immediately recognising the voice of his telephone caller. He didn't attempt to turn round, merely saying – with difficulty as his heart was thumping so painfully – 'All right,' to signify that he understood.

The voice then said: 'I am an initiate of the Friends of Hecate, a group formed in Sussex,' and when Charles asked what sort of group, went on, 'The nearest I can describe our activities to you is that we are followers of Satanism. At every meeting we hold we sacrifice some animal or other. My fellow initiate who is with me tonight will confirm that if you doubt what I say.'

Charles felt he was in no position to disagree with anything that was being said; indeed he began to wonder just how many of them were secreted in the dense foliage, and promptly told the man he didn't doubt him.

The initiate's voice became impassive as he coldly chronicled the vile practices of the cult. 'We hold meetings in Clapham Woods every month, and dogs or other domestic or farm animals are sacrificed. It all depends on what is easy to obtain at the time.'

Trying to keep his voice controlled, Charles asked about the disappearing dogs, and if they were anything to do with the UFOs that had been sighted?

The initiate's reply was swift and terse: 'We have already told you that our cult demands a sacrifice at every meeting,' he stated, continuing, 'You are very close to a site that has been used. But if the weather is bad we make other arrangements.'

Charles then asked how long they had been using the site, and after a brief pause the voice said, 'We have been using this *area* for ten years, and plan to continue using it for another ten, after which time we will select other areas in which to spread the word.'

Before Charles had time to comment, the man went on, 'We use Clapham Wood because it is the most convenient for our members and because the atmosphere of the wood is right for our purposes.'

This time Charles plucked up the courage to ask quickly, 'Exactly what *are* your purposes?' But this, apparently, was too impertinent a question to warrant an answer, and the initiate ignored it by saying instead, sternly, 'There are people in high places holding positions of power and authority who are directly involved and will tolerate no interference.' He paused dramatically before delivering his final grim words: 'We will stop at nothing to ensure the safety of our cult!' Then there was silence.

Charles stood on the pathway straining his ears to catch any sounds of movement or rustling in the bushes or snap of a twig to betray a presence: there was none. The meeting was closed. Charles felt himself dismissed.

With the initiate's ominous warning still ringing in his ears, he walked swiftly away, looking neither to right nor left, but having the strange feeling that he'd been caught up in a time warp, as if the path he was treading had transported him, temporarily, back into another century – into medieval Britain with all its magic, murder and mayhem.

Gaining the dual carriageway with its bright lights and noisy flow of traffic, he found even his credulity was being stretched, realist though he was. Who, in this England of 1978, would believe that such a bizarre meeting had ever taken place? What had been the purpose of it, anyway? Surely not just to acquaint him with the nefarious practices of their cult, or even claim responsibility for the disappearance of the dogs? There had to be another reason.

Charles wondered if word had got around from his Brighton connections that he was interested in the occult, and if so, was he being vetted for possible inclusion in their secret cult? On the other hand, were they just playing on his natural investigative curiosity, perhaps with a view to some ulterior motive later if he didn't heed their warning?

He didn't know what to think, but one thing he did know: his lonely investigations must go on. For only a bare week previously – on the afternoon of Hallowe'en – the Reverend Harry Neil Snelling, retired vicar of Clapham, had gone missing in suspicious circumstances, and despite diligent searching that was still continuing, he had not been found. Suddenly Charles had a grim gut feeling about the fate of the kindly old gentleman. Nothing, he resolved, was going to stop him from seeking out the truth now.

SUSPICIOUS VILLAGERS

Just prior to this, on one Saturday afternoon in late October, I was driving through the Sussex countryside in search of suitable material for inclusion in my 'Moods of Nature' photographic colour series, and pulled into a lay-by on the A 27 a few yards past the Horse & Groom at Patching.

I had not at that time met Charles, let alone become acquainted with any of his Clapham experiences. On this particular occasion I was accompanied by my friend, Tony Jones, a landscape photographer, whom I left in the vicinity of the car while I walked back to an area of interesting landscape I'd seen.

It was one of those warm autumn days, bright and clear, with the sun at a low angle highlighting the multi-coloured foliage against the spacious background of stark ploughed fields. After taking some shots I decided to walk to Patching Hill, and as I was trudging up the increasing gradient of Patching High Street, I suddenly became aware of a strange feeling of hostility on the part of the residents.

Everywhere I looked were watchful eyes. People in their gardens glared at me suspiciously as I passed, my camera slung over my shoulder, some of them even displaying open contempt. In one or two cases, as I smiled and nodded to acknowledge their presence, they deliberately turned away.

Feeling not a little surprised at this reception – and decidedly uneasy – I continued walking as nonchalantly as possible up Patching Hill. On the way back I experienced exactly the same thing: people staring, then pointedly disappearing back into their homes at my approach, their silent, antagonistic behaviour being unlike anything I had ever known before.

Thinking that perhaps I was over-reacting, I returned to my car, to be regaled with an even stranger story from Tony. A police car had pulled up, he said, and an officer had got out and approached him, saying, 'I have been asked to ask you exactly what you're doing.' Somewhat taken aback, Tony nevertheless explained the purpose of our photographic excursion, upon which he replied, 'I suppose that's all right then,' and getting back into his car, promptly drove off.

Thoroughly mystified, we could only think that the Patching residents had taken exception to our cameras, although we were obviously only taking shots of foliage, and certainly had not attempted to photograph anyone or any personal property, such not being our intention anyway. To Tony, an experienced landscape photographer who has travelled all over the United Kingdom and to remote places, the incident was all the more remarkable because he had never before – or since – been questioned by police in this way. Why had the residents been so incensed by our presence that they had to ask the police to investigate us, albeit half-heartedly? What were they afraid of? Why were they so watchful and suspicious? Or what had they got to hide?

In the light of subsequent events and by reason of Patching's close ties with neighbouring Clapham, could it be that their suspicious attitude was not entirely unrelated to the shadowy affairs being spawned in Clapham Wood, and which, through unwelcome publicity, were slowly and surely being brought out into the open?

AFTERMATH OF THE SECRET MEETING

Charles Walker had not long to wait before he realised that the initiate's warning had been no idle threat, for several small mishaps befell him during the weeks following the meeting and he had no doubt at all but that he was being singled out. But he was still obstinately pursuing his investigations when his busy sales job allowed, although he realised the run up to Christmas would greatly curtail his efforts. It was not this, however, that forced him to suspend his activities.

Cycling home from work in the late afternoon of a chill November day, Charles was taking his usual route along Tarring Road, West Worthing. It was 4.45 pm and there were few people about, it being the pre-rush hour and the traffic minimal. Travelling in a westerly direction, he had just passed the traffic lights by West Worthing railway station and was approaching the Grand Avenue T-junction when he heard a car coming up behind him, which suddenly de-throttled. Though slightly muffled, the engine noise was nevertheless distinct, giving Charles the impression that the vehicle intended turning left into Grand Avenue just ahead of him.

At that moment, however, he felt a gigantic bump, and the next thing he knew he was lying flat on his back, his head against the concrete pavement, and his bicycle in a crumpled heap beside him, the car having accelerated down the road out of sight.

Charles never even saw what type of vehicle had hit him, his only memory being of the change in engine pitch. He suffered head and back injuries which left him partially paralysed for many weeks, and it was over two months before he was pronounced well enough to return to work. As may be expected, there were no witnesses to this hit-and-run 'accident'.

DEMONIC MURAL

During the now infamous 'winter of discontent' (1978–9) Charles lay low, but rather than feeling frightened off by events, he was now more than ever determined to find out what was really going on. Nevertheless, he realised that to go too fast too soon could be disastrous, so he waited until the Spring of 1979 before again venturing up to Clapham.

Armed with his camera, he paid a visit on this occasion to the historic little church at Clapham, the thirteenth century Church of the Blessed Virgin Mary, and finding it bereft of visitors for once, spent some time in the peaceful atmosphere. Then he browsed around its diminutive churchyard, where amongst the gravestones a pair of pheasants were engaged in noisy courtship. Southwards, beyond the church's boundary wall, Charles could see the impressive manor house, its uncurtained windows signifying it was still unoccupied, and, next to it, the farm – very much occupied judging by the desultory bovine lowing which was emanating from its direction.

Suddenly Charles noticed the old medieval barn in the grounds of the manor house. It was said to be the oldest building in Clapham, completely square, and with very thick walls, and as he thoughtfully observed it he recalled the initiate's words about their sites: 'If the weather is bad we make other arrangements' – words which he had mulled over many times since, wondering where such a place could be.

Now as he was studying the barn, he noticed that the door was slightly ajar. To Charles it seemed like an invitation, and on a sudden impulse he decided to inspect it. Giving a quick glance round to make sure nobody was about, he shinned over the boundary wall, darted up the manor house drive and, pushing open the barn door, nipped inside.

Quite what he was expecting to find Charles didn't know, but certainly not the hideous and overpowering mural which met his gaze as soon as he entered, being immediately inside the door and filling up the whole of the west wall. (Christian altars are always in the east. Satanism being a reversal of Christianity, its altars are placed in the west.)

In brilliant colours, the painting was of the profile of a huge horned head (measuring about 2 feet 6 inches by 2 feet wide), with a scaly Luciferian body and forked tail, set against a backdrop of vivid flames. The figure was depicted holding a sword and chalice, which is the ancient sign of a fertility cult, the small facial features and large eyes giving the impression of a female. The mural's crude style – it was probably painted in ordinary brush or wax crayon – giving a strong Satanic interpretation.

Charles photographed it and promptly left, only in the nick of time as it happened, for a man appeared shouting angrily and gave chase, and as he was carrying a shot gun Charles didn't stop to argue but hurriedly made off homewards, knowing that now he had proof of the secret cult's existence.

ELYMAS SPEAKS

In 1981, the first of my articles on the enigma of Clapham Wood appeared in the magazine *The Unexplained*, and apparently attracted much interest in occult circles and prompted Charles to renew acquaintance with an old friend of his, the high priest of a Brighton coven, who is known as Elymas.

In discussing my article, it appeared that although leading occultists had been aware of the strange effects people were experiencing at Clapham, they hadn't been aware of the extent of such experiences. Being 'white' witches (those followers of *Wicca* who are mindful of the ecology and whose practices are therefore beneficial), they were concerned that things at Clapham would get out of hand. Elymas spoke for all of them when he said,

'What those who follow the black arts get up to has nothing to do with our ways. When we perform a ritual, we make sure that when we have finished, we remove any elemental we may have raised. It is quite possible that a sensitive person may be able to detect a presence for a limited period after a ritual. The period of time may vary from a few hours to a few weeks, but at no time would we leave any form of presence in an area where we have practised. The risk to those uninitiated who may "stumble" across it is too great. I would not rule out the possibility of someone suffering seriously as a result of coming into contact with such forces.'

When Charles asked him what he knew about the Friends of Hecate, Elymas told him that, apart from realising the existence of the cult, little else was known about them. He added:

'They are, however, a group who know what they are doing, and if they have found an area such as Clapham which they find extremely atmospheric and right for their rituals, then nothing will move them. Such people will do almost anything to protect their site.'

Charles had already found out the truth of this for himself, and Elymas ended with a severe caution:

'If what you say about the woods is true, then you are treading on very dangerous ground. Be careful, be *very* careful, for it is folly to underestimate the power and capability of occult and psychic forces. In the wrong hands they can be extremely dangerous.'

A warning which Charles immediately took to heart, for not only did it behove him to exercise extreme caution, but also made him realise that such powers seemed indeed to be in the wrong hands.

3 HECATE, GODDESS OF THE UNDERWORLD

'But listen! At the very first crack of dawn, the ground
Underfoot began to mutter, the woody ridges to quake
And a baying of hounds was heard through the half-light; the
    goddess was coming,
Hecate!'

Virgil
Aeneid Book VI

THREE-NECKED DEITY

After his disturbing meeting with the initiate of the Friends of
Hecate, one of the first things Charles Walker felt he had to do
was to find out all he could about the Greek deity on whom the
nefarious activities of the cult were obviously based.

Having been asked to meet the unknown man at a crossways
in the woods, he was not at all surprised to find that crossroads
were Hecate's favourite places, that she was known as the
goddess of the parting ways, and for this reason was depicted as
having three heads so that she could look down all three paths
at once. Dante's concept that Satan has three faces in Hell seems
to have originated from the three faces of Hecate.

One of her heads was that of a frenzied bitch, the second a
maned horse, and the third a savage snake. Further, she was
described as 'she who makes dogs shiver', and as he investigated,
Charles was struck more and more by the terrible similarity
between ancient mythology and the reality of what was
happening in present-day Clapham Wood.

ORIGIN AND TITLES

Though a minor Greek goddess of the Pantheon, Hecate (or

Hekate) was nevertheless extremely powerful. It is believed that she came from Caria, a Persian province in West Asia Minor, and was said to be the daughter of Titan Perses and the Titaness Asteria.

She was related to both Apollo and Artemis, whose mother, Leto, was Asteria's sister, and Hecate's name ('Holt' in German) seems to be the feminine form of Hekatos, a title of Apollo's meaning 'the far darter', the meaning of her name being 'she who has power far off'.

By the fifth century BC, Hecate had become identified with both Artemis, 'the chaste moon-goddess', and Diana, 'the many-breasted', therefore becoming the third Greek deity to be associated with the moon. According to Francis King in *Sexuality, Magic and Perversion*, later pagans rationalised the existence of three separate moon-goddesses by arguing that the moon was the symbol of femininity and thus had three aspects: Artemis, corresponding to the young chaste girl; Diana, symbolising the fertile mother, and Hecate, the woman who had passed the menopause, sterile, cold and dark.

As Hecate's parents were both symbols of shining light, however, her lunar connection could have been simply genealogical. Also, she could have become identified with Artemis through their mutual association with dogs, both having packs of hounds, though in Hecate's case they were said to be black, wild and wolf-like.

In whatever manner she became associated with the moon, however, she is chiefly regarded as a divinity of the Underworld. In the infernal regions her authority was considerable, and she was called Prytania of the Dead or the Invincible Queen. Other titles by which she is known are Mistress of Ghosts and Spectres, Goddess of Untimely Deaths, Suicides and Epilepsy, Goddess of the Underworld, Queen of Magic (the blacker the better), and Queen of the Witches.

POWERS AND PREFERENCES
Honoured by Zeus who gave her a portion in the Underworld, the earth, and the air, Hecate was held to be very powerful in all these areas. She could give men riches, victory and wisdom, and sat by kings in judgement, helped speakers in the assembly and granted favours in games, sea-fishing and cattle-breeding. She was goddess of enchantments and magic charms as well as

presiding over purification and expiations, and could be invoked by any who made suitable sacrifices to her. She was renowned for sending demons to earth to torment men, or ghosts from Hades to drive people mad or cause epilepsy by her assaults on them.

The sacrifices made to her were usually of a dog, her favourite animal, and the places she haunted most frequently were crossroads, spots near tombs, or the scenes of crimes.

Known also as 'she who meets', Hecate, as mistress of ghosts and spectres and everything uncanny, was said to appear to travellers and walkers by night in lonely places as a frightening apparition, and to especially haunt the places of those who had died untimely deaths and who could join her host of ghoulish followers in darkness.

THE WILD HUNT

This host, or rout, of followers, was known as the Wild Hunt. With three-faced Hecate – 'dread, pale goddess of death' – in the lead bearing torches which gave a mysterious, unearthly light, and accompanied by her inevitable hounds, the ghostly procession would roam the countryside by night in an orgy of destruction.

The followers were composed of all manner of apparitions, part human, part animal, wild men and women, child-eaters, blood-suckers, murderers and murderesses, all diabolic vassals ready to plunge into any form of mischief, mayhem or malevolent magic their leader might require of them under cover of the hours of darkness.

Sometimes the leader was male, probably Herne the Hunter, who was often associated with the Devil and whose name relates him to 'brightness' and the cult of the moon, as does Hecate's.

Unlike the silence usually associated with apparitions, a cacophony of terrifying sound always accompanied the Wild Hunt: the hissing of many venomous snakes entwined in the goddess's hair, the howling of the long-toothed dogs leaping and snarling at her feet, the ground-trembling thunder of the hoof-like feet of the part-animal followers, and the fear-crazed screams of those innocent night travellers unfortunate enough to witness this frightening rabble from the Underworld.

MANDRAKE

As Goddess of the Underworld, authoress of oppressive dreams, epilepsy and madness, the plant *Mandragora officinarum* is specifically associated with Hecate.

It has always had wide uses. In Persia some three thousand years ago it was used as a surgical anaesthetic, a dried anodyne of mandragora and camphor being reconstituted in boiling water and the steaming sponge held to the patient's nostrils until he slept. The Arabs called its deep golden berries 'Satan's Apples', and its soporific powers are reflected in its name, Mandragora, which comes from the ancient Sanskrit *mandros* – to sleep.

In Palestine, the suffering of crucifixion victims was allayed with a sponge of mandragora, and in *Antony and Cleopatra*, Shakespeare wrote: 'Give me to drink mandragora that I might sleep out this great gap of time.'

Early Christians believed that the forked black root of the mandrake, which grows to about a yard in length and is shaped like a man, was made by God as a 'trial run' before he created Adam.

Its aphrodisiac qualities have always been well-known, and in Genesis Chapter 30 we iearn that Reuben 'went in the days of wheat harvest, and found mandrakes in the field and brought them unto his mother Leah' (Verse 14) and that 'God hearkened unto Leah, and she conceived, and bare Jacob the fifth son' (Verse 17).

Mandrake belongs to the family of poisoners related to the harmless potato, the Solanaceae, which includes deadly nightshade, datura and henbane, and the flesh of its man-shaped root is full of poisons such as tropane alkaloids (atropine, hyoscyamine and mandragorine) which are soporific in small doses, but bring delirium, madness, hallucinations and death if taken in quantity.

In view of the fear with which the root is regarded, it is strange that the plant above ground appears quite innocent-looking, with its dark green leaves spreading out in a flat rosette, and its white flowers delicately tinged with purple. In autumn, the flowers turn into golden berries which carry the heavy scent of musk, but here the innocence ends for it is in the harvesting of the root that, traditionally, great danger ensues.

This, apparently, is because the mandrake shrieks when

pulled from the ground, and any who hear it die painfully shortly afterwards. For this reason a large, starving dog used to be employed. Tied to the strong plant, pieces of meat would be flung in front of the hungry hound, which, in desperately straining forward to reach the food, would thereby uproot the plant.

The harvester would have already repaired to a safe distance, or else stuffed his fingers firmly in his ears so as not to hear the plant's agonised shrieking, and as soon as the dog had died it would be buried in the hole left by the uprooted plant in order to appease the evil spirits which had rushed unsuccessfully to the mandrake's aid.

Botanist Dr Andrew Allen says that in medieval Sussex, mandrake automatically became the witching plant, for it could poison imperceptibly so that men and animals sickened and died, and the root's hallucinogenic alkaloids, when sliced into the witches' cauldron in those days, produced the illusion of flight and shape-shifting.

Even today, the dream-like visions it produces in the mind are believed to have a more potent effect than LSD, for not only does mandragorine increase the body's metabolic rate, but hyoscyamine reputedly stimulates sexual interest, especially that of a brutal nature.

Although native to Mediterranean lands, the male or spring mandrake has been grown in Sussex gardens since Roman times, and Dr Allen believes it still flourishes wild in one or two south-facing nooks on the South Downs. To his special knowledge, one such plant was growing in the woods south of Clapham Village in the 1970s, but suddenly in 1978, he found it had been uprooted.

THE RITES OF HECATE
Apollonius Rhodius described in the *Argonautica* how Aeson's son, Jason, consulted Medea, 'a maiden that uses sorcery under the guidance of Hecate', who advised him that to enlist Hecate's aid he must go alone at night 'clad in dusky raiment' after washing in a river, and dig a rounded pit ('Over the graves of the dead', though this translation does not specifically mention this) in which he had built a fire and slay a sheep to propitiate 'only-begotten Hecate', leaving for her an offering of 'the hive-stored labour of bees'.

When he had sought the grace of the goddess, Medea exhorted Jason to 'retreat from the pyre and let neither the sound of feet drive thee to turn back, nor the baying of hounds, lest haply thou shouldst maim all the rites and thyself fail to return duly to thy comrades'.

Jason did as she bade him, and after calling on Hecate Brimo (Mighty One) to aid him in his contest, he drew back;

'and she heard him, the dread goddess, from the uttermost depths, and came to the sacrifice of Aeson's son; and round her, horrible serpents twined themselves among the oak boughs and there was a gleam of countless torches, and sharply howled around her the hounds of hell. All the meadows trembled at her step; and the nymphs that haunt the marsh and the river shrieked ...'

Despite being afraid, Jason did not turn round but ran until he came back to his comrades. And at dawn he carried out Medea's further instructions, annointing his body with oil so that in it would be 'boundless prowess and mighty strength, and thou wilt deem thyself a match not for men but for immortal gods' and sprinkling his shield and sword, 'whereupon the spear-heads of the earthborn men shall not pierce thee', and emerged from his contest triumphant.

In one of Theocritus's Idylls, Simaetha weaves a love spell to win back her faithless lover, in the course of which she prays to Hecate 'before whom even the dogs stand shivering as she comes over the graves of the dead and the dark blood ...' and apparently her lover returns to her in due time.

Similar descriptions of Hecate's terrifying night-wanderings appear in many ancient passages, from which it can be deduced that her aid was enlisted in the carrying out of many forms of magic, particularly black magic and necromancy.

INVOCATION

Referring again to Francis King's book *Sexuality, Magic and Perversion*, the author says that the terrifying nature of the worship of Hecate can be illustrated by the following invocation of her:

'Come Infernal ... Bombo, Goddess of the broad roadways, of the cross road, thou who goest to and fro at night, torch in hand, enemy of the day, friend and lover of darkness, thou who dost rejoice when the bitches are howling and warm blood is spilled, thou who art walking amid the phantom and in the place of tombs, thou whose thirst is blood, thou who dost strike chill fear into mortal heart, Gorgo, Mormo, Moon (other names for Hecate) of a thousand forms, cast a propitious eye upon our sacrifice.'

EPILOGUE

That invocation, Charles felt, was more than enough to confirm all that he had heard, and gleaned, about Hecate and her followers. But as if he needed more, he came across the following brief sentence in *The World of Witches* by Julio Caro Baroja, published in 1968, wherein the author says of Hecate:

'... she is in fact a deity around whom secret cults and ideas of terror could easily develop.'

Which summed up in a nutshell all that Charles had feared about the secret cult practising in Clapham Wood and calling themselves 'The Friends of Hecate'.

4 *CLAPHAM FROM DOMESDAY*

'Hilltop't Clapham sitteth all replete
Where God and De'il 'tis said doth meet.'

                    Attributed to a Patching cleric, date unknown

THE VILLAGE

It would seem from the above mischievous couplet that the village of Clapham was originally sited on the hill where its church still stands. In fact, the first element of the name Clapham – either 'Clap' or 'Clop' – means 'hill', and the second probably indicates an early Saxon settlement. It was not uncommon for villages to move their positions, a major factor being the onset of the Black Death (bubonic plague) which arrived from the Continent and ravaged England from the fourteenth century, spreading from Weymouth and wiping out half the population of southernmost villages.

Because of infected houses and mass graves, many villages moved more than once, and a former chairman of the parish council at Clapham, Mr Walter Jones, maintained that Clapham had shifted its centre of population on at least three occasions: from its early Saxon hill community to the Holt hamlet and, thirdly, to its present position.

Lying four miles north-west of Worthing on the south slopes of the chalky South Downs, the modern parish of Clapham stretches from north to south with an eastwards extension in its southern precinct. The ancient parish also included two detached parts, one being a dry valley which contained the Shelleys' sheltered residence of Michelgrove, and the other Lee Farm, and both these detached parts were transferred in 1933 to Patching and Angmering respectively.

Dry valleys dissect the northern part of the parish, and meet to form the valley which separates the villages of Clapham and Patching. Running along this valley is the road called Long Furlong, part of which was under the control of the Shelleys who sometimes closed it entirely to the public, on one occasion at least levying a toll of a penny, and the old castellated tollhouse still stands at the foot of the South Downs along this road at Clapham.

The Long Furlong road was incorporated in the public turnpike road between Findon and Littlehampton in 1823. At the same time the Michelgrove – Findon road was closed as a public carriageway, and the Long Furlong road (the A 280) disturnpiked in 1878.

At its southern end, the parish of Clapham is crossed by the Chichester – Brighton road, which is of great antiquity, and is now the A 27 dual carriageway.

The parish lies on chalk, overlaid in its southerly aspect by later deposits on which are Clapham Common and the brick-works. A large proportion of the locality is woodland, the place-names of Holt, Lee and Michelgrove all suggesting settlement in woodland.

The village consists of a single street which climbs eastwards out of the valley, levels out, with a steep drop southwards and a more gradual one eastwards. Both the church and the manor house (formerly Clapham Farm) are situate on rising ground to the north, some distance from the rest of the village. The house is of brick with hung tiles and dates probably from the sixteenth century. An imposing, if elongated structure, it was re-roofed in the late seventeenth century when two tall external chimneys were added. North of the house is a square dovecot of flint rubble with sandstone quoins and walls four feet thick, which is said to be medieval in origin. Used recently for storage of farm materials, this is the 'barn' in which Charles Walker photographed the demonic mural.

The village street is lined both sides with charming and varied types of houses, amongst which is the village shop and post office. There are two hollow oaks in Clapham which have always attracted attention, one being at the entrance to the village's single street, dwarfing a signpost indicating 'Clapham Village' and a notice warning casual visitors there is 'No Through Road', and the other being located east of the parish church.

Whilst many people consider the hollow oak at Clapham's entrance lends a romantic, 'olde worlde' appeal to this pretty downland village, others have said they find its stark bare trunk and spikey branches somewhat forbidding, 'as if the residents don't want strangers', was how one visitor described her feelings about it.

The other hollow tree is Clapham's famed Sentinel Oak, which stands on rising ground belonging to farmer Boaz Cornford, just east of the church. Reputed to be some 700 years old, it has few branches and a man can stand within its hollow trunk. It is believed that where the tree stands was the centre of an ancient village, and this theory is supported by the fact that an earthwork surrounds the parish church.

The earthwork could have druidic connections, the oak being their most venerated tree (the very name 'druid' comes from 'derwydd', Celtic, der, superior; wydd, priest or instructor) and the presence of such a large old oak in the proximity of an earthwork is usually thought to indicate that the site was a sacrificial grove.

In the east part of the parish is the settlement of Holt, which was described as being a 'vill' (a feudal territorial unit or manor) in 1415. The present Holt Farm is converted from three brick cottages dated 1851, and there are a couple of seventeenth century houses also further to the north, but after 1816 virtually the whole area became part of the Michelgrove estate.

In the south-east corner of the parish of Clapham, but quite a walk from the village, stands the Coach and Horses Inn, which was newly built in 1741 when it was called the Rose and Crown. In 1779 it was known as the half-way house between Arundel and Shoreham.

North of the village there are disturbances in the ground, thought to indicate the presence of a Black Death mass grave though no record seems to exist of this, and also a large round pit whose origin is unknown. Tentative suggestions, however, have been put forward that it is either a crater caused by a meteorite which hit Clapham in the distant past, or the result of a war-time bomb, an ancient lime pit, or a UFO landing site! But no-one has come up with an acceptable explanation and the pit remains something of a mystery.

Also in this area is a network of old paths, but in this case there is no doubt as to their origin, for local archaeologists and historians are quite sure they are the former streets of a settlement once sited on this hill.

There have been a number of Roman and medieval finds of pottery and flint in the area, those north of Clapham on Black Patch hill being dated between the second and fourth centuries, and one item found at Harrow Hill (whose top is scheduled as an ancient monument) being a pre-Roman saddle quern used for grinding corn. The whole corner of a large house, believed to have been built in Roman times, and which included an oven, was found during a dig west of the picturesque pond at Patching.

The affairs of Clapham cannot be entirely divorced from those of its neighbour, Patching, divided though they are by the lovely valleyed road of Long Furlong. If one thinks of this road, northwards from the A 27, as the spine of an open book, the right-hand page is Clapham, the left-hand page, Patching. But here the analogy ends, for so many intrigues litter their chequered histories that far from being an open book, a cloak of secrecy seems to have enshrouded both villages down the centuries. Even today their tenuous, geographically-determined union seems beset by suspicion, as if the ancestral shades from a diabolic past haunt them still.

MANOR OF CLAPHAM

The Manor of Clapham was held of King Edward by one Alwin in 1066, but in 1073 it belonged to William de Braose as part of what became the honor of Bramber, to which it later belonged.

Amongst those who are recorded as having held the Manor of Clapham are Gilbert St Owen and his heirs for 300 years, the le Fauconers, who later adopted the name of le Michelgrove, and John Wood and his heirs, who sold it to Sir William Shelley, Lord of the Manor of Michelgrove, in 1527, the Michelgrove family estates having passed to the Shelley family in 1474 on Elizabeth le Michelgrove's marriage to John Shelley.

Michelgrove was described in 1193 as being an outlying settlement. Previously, in 1086, it was probably represented by the 'two hides belonging to Clapham Manor' in Domesday, which were in the Rape of Roger de Montgomery, but by 1242 Michelgrove was recorded as being held in the Rape of Bramber. After Sir William Shelley became Lord of the Manor of Clapham in 1527, the two manors descended together, Michelgrove eventually becoming absorbed in Clapham.

The controversial Shelleys had held the manor for 300 years until Sir John Shelley sold the Michelgrove estates (which by then included the greater part of the Parish) to Richard Walker of Liverpool, who died the following year, and his son Richard Watt Walker, who apparently didn't come of age until 1813, lived so extravagantly that he had to sell the estate in 1827 to Bernard Edward, Duke of Norfolk.

In 1843–4 practically the whole parish was in the duke's possession, although by 1874 a later duke exchanged 400 acres in the east and south of the main part of the parish with Lady Burrell, widow of Sir Percy Burrell, Baronet, of Castle Goring, and from her the lands passed to her sister, Adelaide Harriet, who married Sir Alfred Somerset, also of Castle Goring. In the 1920s more of the parish, including Clapham Farm, passed from the Duke of Norfolk's estate to the Castle Goring estate, and has remained in the Somerset family ever since.

Perhaps the best-known of the Somersets was Mr Cecil Somerset, whose full names were Arthur Plantagenet Francis Cecil Somerset (1889–1957) the son of Colonel Sir Alfred and Lady Somerset who were cousins, and who was born at Castle Goring. Mr Somerset owned Castle Goring estate, which consists of about 2,500 acres of downlands and woods including Clapham Woods, and he lived in Castle Goring until it was taken over by the military in 1940 and subsequently sold.

A popular figure and keen cricketer, he was also fond of shooting and intended at one time to go deer-stalking. He was sole patron of the living at Angmering, and was joint patron, with the Archbishop of Canterbury, of the living of St Mary's Church at Clapham where he was for many years a churchwarden.

He is remembered chiefly for sending a gift to Marshal Stalin in 1943 – with Whitehall's approval – of what was believed to be the only known portrait of Peter the Great of Russia, painted by Ludolph Backhuysen, the famous Dutch marine artist, at Saardam, Holland, in 1697. Mr Somerset's son-in-law, then Commander Palmer, RN, delivered this unique painting as a gesture of goodwill to the Russian people in honour of their fight against the German Army during World War 2, but it is believed Stalin declined it. This Saardam portrait of Peter the Great was formerly one of the treasures of St Petersburg, where it was housed for two hundred years, but it went missing from Russia for a quarter of a century, eventually being recovered in London. It was given to Mr Cecil Somerset's father by a relative of the famous Tsar Nicholas, and the portrait had graced the walls of Castle Goring for thirty years until removed and stored with other treasures for safe keeping during the war.

Castle Goring, a notable land-mark and one of Worthing's showpieces, has been variously described as a 'freak mansion', 'the house with two faces' and 'a highly individual example of architectural schizophrenia', for it appears to be two houses in one: from the south it is built in the Palladian style after a villa in Rome designed by Biagio Rebecca, and from the north it is castellated like a miniature Arundel Castle, on part of which it was said to have been planned.

Built by eccentric Sir Bysshe Shelley for his grandson, Percy Bysshe Shelley, the poet, work started on it towards the end of the eighteenth century but was not completed by Sir Bysshe's death although he had by that time already spent some one hundred thousand pounds on it. In 1816 the property was put up for auction but not sold, it being described then as being unfinished and uninhabitable. But in 1824 Sir Timothy Shelley leased it to Captain Pechell for a yearly rent of £20 on condition that he repaired the building, and he remained in tenancy until 1845 when the land and buildings were sold to him by Mary Shelley, widow of the poet (who, incidentally, had never lived in it) and her son, Sir Percy Florence Shelley, 3rd Baronet.

A house at Michelgrove was mentioned in 1279, and was rebuilt by Sir William Shelley in 1534. The Tudor building was quadrangular, with an open internal courtyard and polygonal towers. It was of brick and the south entrance facade had a three-bay Doric or Tuscan arcade, believed to be of stone. A gallery on the first floor was 78 feet long and the house was said to contain 50 rooms. During the mid-eighteenth century extensive alterations were made and the building was cased in cream-coloured bricks and boasted four square towers. Further embellishments were added on its sale to the Walker family including a groined chestnut ceiling to the drawing room which measured 46 feet by 40 feet, and a very elaborate staircase which was later moved to Burton Park, near Petworth. Large stables were also added, and a former pigeon-house which stood on a hill to the south was converted into a clocktower, subsequently falling into disrepair and being demolished in 1974.

The park belonging to the house lay to the south almost entirely in Angmering parish, and contained 649 deer at the count in 1802. When Richard Watt Walker sold Michelgrove to the Duke of Norfolk, the duke immediately gave orders to have the house demolished, but as previously mentioned, the old castellated toll-house was left untouched, and was recently made into a unique cottage without losing its intrinsic character of a tollgate, which, as Raymond Hodges-Paul describes it, 'is the last remaining local relic of a bygone age, when the coaches reigned supreme on the Sussex roads and the turnpike keeper was probably as much abused as are some of today's traffic wardens!'

One of these historic coaches was named 'The Champion' and belonged to the Walker brothers (Richard Watt Walker, and John Walker, sons of Richard Walker of Liverpool), who started up the coach service in competition with their enemy, George Cross, who ran Cross's Coaches and owned a fast coach called 'The Comet'. This coach took a route to London via Arundel, down Bury Hill to Pulborough, and thence joining the Worthing to London road at Bear Green. The Walker brothers, on the other hand, decided to shorten the route by making a turnpike road from Clapham and Patching to Findon, and thereafter joining the Worthing to London road; and the brothers used Michelgrove's double lodge as the tollgate for the turnpike. The turnpike road is now known as Long Furlong, in the making of which they removed some important standing stones from the area, which has, according to ley and standing stone enthusiasts, interfered with the earth current and had a deleterious effect on the whole area.

Despite using splendid teams of horses and inducing customers to use their coaches by providing additional comforts, the Walker brothers were not able to take away Cross's customers, and finally, in 1828, the brothers went broke and thus were forced to sell Michelgrove to the Duke of Norfolk. It was later said that one of them became an ostler at an inn whose landlord had once been his own butler, and the son of a former Rector of Patching placed on record other freak escapades and ignominies of the two brothers, whom he described as being a 'wild couple'.

Patching, incidentally, was renowned for its truffles, and a professional truffle hunter by the name of William Leach, who

48

came over from the West Indies in the early nineteenth century seeking this delicacy (*Lycoperdon tuber*), found a plentiful supply at Patching, where he promptly settled.

Down the centuries the histories of Clapham and Patching have developed in tandem. In Domesday we read:

'The Archbishop holds Patchinges. It was always appropriated to clothe the monks. In the demesne are two ploughs and twenty-two villeins and twenty-one bondsmen having six ploughs ... Here is a church and Wood for pannage (feeding) for four hogs.'

In the same Domesday survey, Clapham has only 'five villeins and eight bondsmen' but its population increased whilst Patching's declined, both villages running neck-and-neck in 1891 with 270 inhabitants each.

But, divisive though some of their historical events may have been, Clapham and Patching shared a common benefactor: the Shelleys of Michelgrove, upon whom both villages were largely dependent and who did so much towards the upkeep of their respective churches that these twin downland villages are said to possess one of the finest collections of church plate in the county.

CLAPHAM CHURCH

The first rector of the Church of the Blessed Virgin Mary at Clapham was William de Radenore in 1257, from which date the list of rectors is continuous. Clapham was apparently a parish by 1073 when William de Braose gave tithes from it to his college at Bramber, and the existing church is believed to include late eleventh century work. A skull found under the western pillar of the north arcade during restoration in 1910 (and which was left undisturbed in its resting-place) is believed to have lain there for a thousand years. In the churchyard, just to the right on entering the lych-gate, is a gravestone bearing a cross nearly 5 feet high, and this is certainly not later than the twelfth century and is very probably earlier.

The church is a very small, compact building of flint and stone dressings, with a chancel, aisled nave and a north-west tower which has a simple pyramidal cap. Of an irregular shape, the building is nevertheless an attractive one, redolent in its timeless setting of by-gone ages and centuries of dignified worshippers who would have strolled up the winding hill path to their church, uncluttered by the pressures of the modern day, although religious persecution seems to have been an ever-present harassment.

Although its southern and eastern aspects are open, it is overshadowed on its northern and western boundaries by the tall, dense trees of Clapham Wood, with which it not only seems to blend in snugly, but whose towering presence serve the more to emphasise this tiny church's four-square strength and solidarity. There are, however, those who find the very proximity of these woods disquieting, one parishioner remarking that he felt they were 'encroaching like triffids on God's Small Acre', whilst another likened the creeping, overhanging wood-land north-west of the church (where the mysterious pit is situate) to 'walking through cobwebs in darkness'.

The church was dedicated in 1406, and the first thing noticed on entering the west door is that the chancel is not in a straight line with the nave but faces considerably to the northward. Other ancient churches of irregular shape – many dedicated, like Clapham Church, to St Mary or St Margaret – are similarly laid out: this is not uncommon and was very probably done deliberately to represent the angle of the Lord's head on the Cross, although there seems to be no authority for this theory.

The Reformation appears to have been strongly resisted in Clapham; John Wall (rector from 1531–59) adhered to the old faith and his successor David Spencer was reported in 1569 to be refusing to preach the new doctrines. Ten years later, after Spencer's death, the churchwardens were themselves presented for refusing to present recusants.

Numerous recusants were recorded in Clapham, including many members of the Shelley family, among them two school masters, and William Shelley of Michelgrove was himself imprisoned for recusancy in 1580.

As with all ancient churches, its history is attended by religious persecution, the Roman Catholic leanings of the sixteenth century being succeeded in the next century by equally strong Protestant leanings. In 1635, Rector Henry Nye was inhibited from preaching by the vicar-general on suspicion on Puritanism. Seven years later he was appointed a member of the Westminster Assembly of Divines, and his successors at

Clapham, Andrew and Samuel Wilmer, were members of a notable Puritan family.

Samuel, however, seems to have been a Congregationalist, because his parishioners drew attention to his zeal in 'gathering the scattered saints into one body to enjoy gospel ordinances' when they petitioned in 1653 that he should be granted the living at Patching in addition to Clapham. He was nevertheless ejected from Patching at the Restoration and forfeited Clapham in 1662 for failure to comply with the Act of Uniformity. His successor, a former Royalist soldier, brought the parish back to orthodoxy.

In 1676 a religious census in Clapham showed 96 conformists and 14 papists and no non-conformists, and 100 years later all the families in the parish were church families except for one baptist!

Religious friction between Clapham and Patching continued under the 50-year tenure of rector William Norse, who dominated the two churches, and by 1850 (when hymn singing was at last introduced at Clapham) it came to a head when the elderly rector of Patching, Edmund Tew, complained that his parishioners were being enticed away – possibly by the Duke – and this led to the union of the two benefices in 1888.

Extensive restoration of Clapham church was undertaken by Sir Gilbert Scott in 1873–4, and the three lancet windows on the western wall of the nave are largely his work. The arcading here differs in design on opposite sides, showing the evolution of Transitional Norman work to Early English, but externally the appearance of the church has changed little since the end of the twelfth century.

An interesting feature is that the fifteenth century north door has been walled up, and whilst it is not known when this was done, the reason for it is more than likely to have been as a precaution against witchcraft.

The north has always been the traditional source of mystic energy, and for thousands of years it was believed that all occult power came from Hyperborea, 'the land beyond the north wind'. In medieval times reluctant Christians would gather round the north side of churches to chant hymns to their forbidden gods, and even orthodox believers were wary of the north side, the only graves found there usually being those of suicides or murderers. In order to prevent the entrance of evil spirits, therefore, it was the clergy's practice to permanently seal the north doors, and this was obviously the case at Clapham.

The church's three historic bells are believed to date from 1315 and to be cast by founder Nicholas le Rous of London. They comprise the earliest ring of three in Great Britain, and are named Jacobus, Caterina and Caterina Margarita.

In the south wall is a narrow window said to be a leper's window though this is controversial. However, it is a fact that nearby Lee Farm was once a medieval leper settlement, and even today older inhabitants of the village refer to a path leading from the farm to the church as 'Leper's Path'.

On the inside, a circular engraving on a thirteenth century pillar on the eastern face of the south aisle is said to be a sundial, with six lines, or rays, emanating from a central indentation, but it could be the old Celtic rune for 'light'. Whilst the central indentation could indicate the gnomon's position, at the same time it is well-known that great cunning was employed in the craftsmanship of many such ancient marks whose meanings were intended to be twofold: one to serve the devout church-goers, and the other to satisfy the paganistic element who only attended church under duress. It could therefore be a rune made to look like a sundial.

Runes, a sacred alphabet of mystical symbols, still used today in one form or another by modern practitioners of *Wicca* (the witches' term for their craft), each possess a double meaning in themselves, more properly referred to as an 'inner and outer breath'. Germanic in origin, the rune for 'Sig' (sun) was used by the Nazis, who were heavily involved in the occult, as a collar flash on uniforms of the feared 'SS', and as far back as the early thirteenth century, a Germanic group of Satanist heretics called Luciferans worshipped 'the light bearer' (another concept of this symbol) who they believed would defeat God and regain heaven and so take up his rightful place as creator of the world.

The inner meaning of this symbol is, in fact, 'winning' or 'victory', a very powerful reason for its adoption by the Nazis in this way, and in her book *Witchcraft for Tomorrow*, Doreen Valiente comments on runic influences and says 'One wonders whether perhaps the centuries-old magical potency of these things which he (Hitler) tried to steal worked against him in the end.'

As many Christian churches were built on what were

formerly pagan sacred sites, connotations of witchcraft are not unusual, and three lines representing the footprint of the sacred night owl are often found on church walls. This symbol was used historically as the mark of the Free French in World War 2, and today is known more widely as the logo of the Campaign for Nuclear Disarmament, which, if the peaceful aura within Clapham church's ancient walls is any indication, would seem particularly apt.

CURSES, CRIMES AND OCCULT CONNECTIONS

History records that the Rape of Bramber in general and Clapham village in particular, were the subject, in medieval times, of two potent curses, one uttered by a descendant of William de Braose, the other by Robert le Fauconer.

William de Braose was granted the Rape of Bramber in 1073, but held it for only 30 years, being deposed by Henry the First who gave the land to Gilbert St Owen, a man who, by all early accounts, was greatly feared and 'ruled with mace and lance'. Though angered by his unfair treatment and total rejection by the new monarch, de Braose could do nothing but retire to his northern estates, where, so far as is known, he was left in peace. It was his descendants who felt the full wrath of the Plantagenet Kings – the notorious John in particular – who reigned from 1199 – 1216.

The name Plantagenet derives from the sprig of broom *Planta genista* worn in the helmets of the fearless Dukes of Anjou in battle, and adopted as their badge by Geoffrey the Handsome, the Angevin who fathered England's Henry II and who was more commonly known by his preferred title of 'Plantagenet'.

In her book *The God of the Witches*, Dr Margaret Murray expounds a theory that links the Plantagenet dynasty through its dark Angevin history with the very roots of European witchcraft, for whilst most of Europe had converted to Christianity, the Germans held fast to their paganistic beliefs, and the Angevin dynasty was said to have been born from a long line of pagans.

Although the legendary father of the race was the Breton woodsman known as Tortulf the Forester, half-brigand, half-hunter, an outlaw of almost supernatural strength who won many broad lands along the Loire, historically the first Count of

Anjou was his descendant, Fulk the Red, who had attached himself to the Dukes of France and been rewarded with the County of Anjou.

The most notorious of the Angevins according to historian J.R. Green was his grandson, Fulk the Black, who was 'the first in whom we can trace that marked type of character which their House was to preserve with a fatal constancy through two hundred years'. That 'type of character' was one of unadulterated evil.

Devoid of any natural affection, Fulk the Black had a wife burnt at the stake, which celebration it is said he dressed himself in his best clothes to enjoy, and familiar though the age was with cruelty in all its many forms, his monstrous crimes terrified everyone, including the French king. His 50-year reign of barbarity ended with his death in 1040, by which time Fulk the Black had made Anjou the greatest province in France.

Although William the Conqueror temporarily halted the advance of the House of Anjou, it woke to fresh energy in the early twelfth century with the accession of Fulk of Jerusalem, who was the one enemy that Henry the First of England feared above all others.

In order to disarm his restless hostility, King Henry gave to Fulk's son, Geoffrey the Handsome, the hand in marriage of his widowed daughter, Matilda. It was a disastrous union shrouded in secrecy from the beginning, and as history records, it brought civil war and great trouble to this country, thus setting the scene for the years of misrule and disorder that followed this dubious French connection.

Henry II, who added Aquitaine and Gascony to the Angevin Empire in France but who is remembered chiefly for ordering the murder of Becket, Archbishop of Canterbury, in 1170, was the son of Geoffrey, Duke of Anjou, and Matilda, and the first of the Plantagenets.

His two sons were Richard the First and John – in whom, particularly, the Angevin characteristic of unbridled cruelty seems to have reigned supreme, although both brothers had violent tempers and by their monstrous behaviour caused St Bernard, Cistercian Abbot of Clairvaux in France, to say of them: 'From the devil they came and to the devil they shall return', a sentiment echoed by many at the time, including, no doubt, William de Braose's descendant of the same name.

Cheated, as he had been, out of inheriting the Rape of Bramber, de Braose had ample reason to hate Henry the First's grandsons, and this turned to fear when John came to the throne in 1199 because John's merciless military governor, Horace de Paschal, overlord of a personal army of Welsh and Flemish mercenaries, held the manor adjacent to William de Braose's northern estates.

History records that no-one was safe from this man. Outrage followed outrage, especially when King John ordered that his most powerful barons – de Braose included – were to give up their youngest child as hostage to ensure their good behaviour, Horace de Paschal being made hostage collector; and when John personally hanged 28 boys at Nottingham Court in 1212, everyone realised he meant what he said. William de Braose, fearful for the safety of his only son, endeavoured to hide both him and the boy's mother, but to no avail. John had them flung into a dungeon where they eventually starved to death in the most horrifying circumstances.

Beside himself with anger and grief, de Braose, who no longer had any military power, could only call down all the demonic hell he could muster on King John's head. He cursed the Plantagenets, the monarchy, the aristocracy and, above all, the Rape of Bramber, which was a favourite hunting ground of John and his bestial followers. The words he uttered were:

'I call upon the Damned to likewise damn the Bramber Woods of Suosexe, and may John and his creed ne'er walk in peace.'

The curse uttered against Clapham village was over a trivial matter but obviously none the less meaningful at the time. It was made by Robert le Fauconer after losing a case he'd brought against Parson Adam le Gest for allegedly causing him bodily harm at Clapham, which was recorded at Chichester Assizes in 1288 (extracted from Cartwright's *Rape of Bramber 1820*). Not only did the Jury acquit the priest after he had successfully pleaded his innocence of any such alleged violence, but they further amerced le Fauconer for making a false charge. Le Fauconer promptly cursed Clapham:

'I call upon She who knows to damn this accursed village and all its meagre holdings. May the priesthood of this false God soon come to know their fate.'

In the light of subsequent events, this curse seems to have had a powerful effect on the priesthood and far-reaching results in Clapham.

Robert le Fauconer died in 1302, and it was his son and heir, John, who some ten years later, assumed the name of de Michelgrove.

John de Michelgrove's great-great-granddaughter, Elizabeth de Michelgrove, married John Shelley, and that the Shelleys were no strangers to curses and crimes is obvious from even a brief glance at their family history. John was beheaded when Henry IV came to the throne in 1399 for 'following the fortunes of Richard II' and despite many members of this large family attaining high office, there seem to be quite a few skeletons in the historic cupboard, at least so far as the Michelgrove branch of the family is concerned.

Sir William Shelley, first son of Sir John Shelley of Michelgrove, succeeded him in 1527 and during the same year bought the Manor of Clapham. He 'found favour' with Henry VIII whom he entertained at Michelgrove, but possibly the King made only this one visit to Clapham. Sir William was later made a Judge of Common Pleas and Recorder of London.

His two brothers, Edward and Richard, founded the Warminghurst and Patcham branches of the family respectively. Sir William was succeeded in 1549 by his son John, who unhappily died the following year, being himself succeeded by his son, also John, who was created a baronet in 1611 and became ancestor of the Maresfield Shelleys.

Reverting to the Michelgrove branch of the family, William Shelley, son of John, was described in 1564 as being 'a misliker of religion'. Recusancy, the practice of religious dissent usually applied to Roman Catholics for refusing to attend Church of England services when it was made legally compulsory so to do, was a common enough crime in those days, and in 1580 William was imprisoned for being a recusant. Many other members of the family suffered similarly, but William seems to have been more of a rebel than the others, for it was he who, in 1586, entered into one of the many Roman Catholic plots to oust Elizabeth from the English throne in favour of Mary, Queen of Scots, in this case Throckmorton's Plot. In Patching Woods, by night, he kept an assignation with a man named Charles Paget, but the pair of conspirators were caught, although some records say that Paget got away and fled to France, and William Shelley was attainted in 1586–7 for his part in the plot. Sentence of death, however, was commuted, and he was released from the Tower in 1596.

In 1635 two more Shelleys, both schoolmasters, were tried for heresy and in the same year only the King's Favour saved Sir John and Lady Shelley from being charged with 'adverse disbelief' – an accusation that bordered on witchcraft and could have had dire results if proven against them. In 1716 another Sir John Shelley publicly decried Roman Catholicism, although five years later he declared 'the Church of England is an affront to all decent Catholics', a turncoat attitude probably forced upon him as much by the religious unrest of the times as by the whole family's seeming aversion to any religious conformity.

The most famous of the Shelleys was, of course, the poet Percy Bysshe Shelley, described by Robert Southey, the historian and poet, as 'a Satanist, schooled in the Black Arts by his accursed forefathers'. To Southey, both Shelley and Byron were from 'the Satanic School', and certainly Shelley's preoccupation with all things occult warranted such a designation.

Archibald T. Strong echoed Southey's view when he wrote in *Three Studies of Shelley*:

'... We now pass to another class of abnormality in Shelley's spiritual vision, and one which has a direct relation to certain elements in his poetry. From earliest childhood he had taken the liveliest interest in the supernatural. "Sometimes", Hogg tells us, "he watched the livelong night for ghosts", and his researches into electricity and galvanism, which were to be resumed so ardently in his Oxford days, were varied by the eager perusal of volumes on magic and witchcraft ... and he even tried to raise a ghost himself, uttering incantations and drinking thrice out of a human skull (or its substitute) as he bestrode a running stream. Hogg informs us that even at Oxford Shelley had "a decided inclination for magic, daemonology, incantations, raising the dead, evoking spirits and devils, seeing ghosts, and chatting familiarly with apparitions".'

(Thomas Jefferson Hogg, Shelley's friend and fellow Oxford student who shared his 'sceptical opinions'.)

In 1811 Shelley was sent down from Oxford for his pamphlet *Necessity of Atheism* which was later printed by the Worthing printers, C. & W. Phillips, despite their receiving a 'friendly hint' from an Oxford booksellers warning them 'of the dangerous tendency of disseminating such vile principles' and the liability they ran of prosecution by the Attorney-General. Every copy in their possession, they said, had been destroyed, but the Worthing company went ahead with printing, probably because Miss Philadelphia Phillips, daughter of the printer, was on good terms with Shelley, who frequently visited the printing works and may even have set up some of the type.

Using the pseudonym 'Jeremiah Stukeley', Shelley sent copies of his pamphlet to every bishop in the United Kingdom and to many other dignitaries, but today there appear to be only two copies of this highly controversial pamphlet in existence.

With Nietzche, Shelley defined Christianity as 'the religious expression of the slave-spirit in man', and although so many of his brilliant works reflected his daring and unorthodox opinions (e.g. *The Masque of Anarchy*, an indictment on Castlereagh, and *The Cenci*, a play on evil, to name but two) he also produced such romantic lyrics as *To a Skylark* and *Ode to the West Wind*. How apt, indeed, was Castle Goring, the architecturally schizophrenic house which his grandfather, Sir Bysshe, had built for him, for Shelley's youthful genius, too, seems to have been split by a kind of poetic schizophrenia.

His first wife committed suicide, and Mary, his second, seems to have been much more of a kindred spirit, sharing with her husband and their friend, Lord Byron, many occult discussions far into the night. It was she who wrote the legend of Frankenstein.

Throughout Shelley's short life there were many strange and ironic connections. For instance, the character in his play, *The Witch of Atlas*, was named Ariel, an impish creature who travels about in a magic boat and is given to playing tricks with the natural world. Shelley named his own boat *Ariel*, but there the poet's magic seems to have deserted him. On 8 July 1822 in the Gulf of Spezia, Italy, he was returning home to his villa at Lerici when a sudden storm sprang up, and although it lasted only 20 minutes, in that brief time the *Ariel* disappeared beneath the waves, taking Shelley with it, his body being washed up ten days later at Via Reggio.

When Shelley's close friend, John Trelawney, who lived in a house of that name in Sompting, Worthing, died aged 90 in

1881, it was said the garden contained a cypress tree which Trelawney had brought back from Shelley's grave in Rome. It was not the only sepulchral connection with Shelley, for after the poet's tragic death, strangely enough his heart wouldn't burn with the rest of the remains at the funeral pyre at Via Reggio, despite being doused in gallons of wine. Witnessed by John Trelawney, Lord Byron and Leigh Hunt among others, the heart was accordingly rescued from the ashes, placed in a small casket and given to Shelley's widow, Mary.

Rumour has it that shortly after this – though how the tale originated is not known – 'a black object in an ornate receptacle' was ceremoniously buried in the woodlands surrounding Castle Goring, in the Manor of Clapham.

As mentioned in Chapter 1, there have been many fires in the Clapham area and thousands of pounds of damage done over the years, but no suspected arsonist was ever brought to justice. Additionally, over a 20-year period, mystery surrounds two major fires, one being Dulaney House (which belonged to the Duke of Norfolk) at Patching, and the other, Clapham Brickworks. Both these large properties were well alight before firemen were called to them, in each case about 6 o'clock on a Saturday morning. No satisfactory cause was ever found.

During the past century several crimes have been recorded including a Jack Upperton who robbed the mail and was gibbeted at a nearby crossroads; a relative of his bearing the same name who murdered a maidservant at Lee Farm whose skeletal remains were found beneath an ancient pathway at Michelgrove; and smuggler James Ruff, who died in the village of Clapham in 1862. He had been engaged in a 'famous smuggling transaction near Worthing on a dirty November night in 1824 involving 300 tubs of spirits', but the deal had gone wrong and in the ensuing fight with blockademen, Ruff had had his nose partially severed by a cutlass, although it was strapped up and apparently grew back on again.

There are many more such tales and interesting characters – too many to detail here – but mention must be made of the miserable miller of Patching, who lived to the south of the village on Highdown Hill and was so melancholy he thought about little else than his own death. He built his own tomb and kept his coffin at his bedside so that he could roll into it when the time came. But that wasn't until 1793, when he was 84 years old, and his tomb on Highdown Hill is a well-known landmark today.

Turning to occult connections, the original *Book of Shadows*, said to contain the entire magical knowledge of the Roman philosopher and magician, Maximus, is believed to be connected with Clapham. This book includes the most secret Rites of Hecate which Maximus was adept at performing, and was brought to Britain by his devotees after the fall of Rome, Maximus having bequeathed it to his friend and fellow magician, Ellysio. The book is recorded as having safely reached our shores in AD 484, and although its actual whereabouts remain a mystery, scholars believe it is still somewhere in Southern England, for Ellysio reputedly lived in a hilly coastal settlement in Regnian Province, the Roman name for Sussex.

The Golden Calf legend is also associated with Sussex. Worshipped by heretics, this idol was brought to Britain in AD 41 by St Paul and supposedly buried at a pagan hilltop site known only to the Keepers of the Faith. When the Romans arrived some three years later, mentions were made in their despatches of this fact, and from their own military movements of that time, it would seem the coastal region of Sussex would have been the most likely resting place for the Golden Calf, especially somewhere like Clapham which was known to have been a Saxon hilltop settlement.

However, there is less evidence to support this assumption than there is regarding the whereabouts of the *Book of Shadows*, and even 500 years later, documentation of any specific event is not easy to come by. Nevertheless, there have been times when such welcome verification was forthcoming after patient research, as happened in the case of Lady Alice le Kyteler, who was indicted by the bishop of Ossory as a witch in 1324 at Kilkenny, Ireland.

Described as being an 'Invoker of Satan at crossroads', Lady Alice had been heard to mutter when her son, William's, fortunes were fading:

'Into the house of William, my son,
Hie all the wealth of Kilkenny Towne.'

Despite her obvious guilt as revealed at the trial, Lady Alice was discharged from custody because she was of such social standing that the magistrates thought it politically dangerous to impose any sentence upon her, and according to Doreen Valiente in *Where Witchcraft Lives*, the bishop of Ossory was placated in his endeavours by having Lady Alice's waiting-woman, Petronilla, burned at the stake instead.

Lady Alice and her son were assisted by some of the nobility who had opposed the bishop to escape across the Irish Sea to England, and were known to have landed somewhere along the Yorkshire coast.

Twenty miles inland is the village of Clapham, Yorkshire, and in about the mid-fourteenth century, a Dame Alice Ketyll and her son, John de Clopham, had to flee for their lives when the villagers rose up against them over some occult malpractice. It is reported that John de Clopham was heir to the title of Regent of Clapham in Clapham Castle, Yorkshire, and that his mother, Dame Alice Ketyll, was an Invoker of Satan. She had been overheard to mumble when the de Clophams fell on bad times:

'Into the house of John, my son,
Hie all the wealth of Clapham towne.'

After which, as with William le Kyteler, John de Clopham became rich again.

When the couple fled from the Yorkshire Clapham, they left John de Clopham's bastard son, Andrew, in the care of friends, and were apparently not heard of again in Yorkshire, but there is strong evidence they came south to the Clapham in Sussex.

Whilst it seems highly probable that Lady Alice le Kyteler and Dame Alice Ketyll were one and the same person, and that William le Kyteler and John de Clopham likewise, there is no actual proof of this. It was known that Lady Alice had many friends amongst the nobility which included the Shelleys, but this social link is not strong enough of itself to connect the Yorkshire village of Clapham with the Sussex village of Clapham, even given the undeniable fact that the people concerned were all interested in the black arts.

However, in the archives of Chichester Reference Library there is a Deed of Estate dated March 26 1411 in which a grant of land was made by one Ralph de Sancto Audeons to Andrew, son of John de Clopham at La Holta, in Clapham, Sussex.

La Holta is now Holt Farm, home of the Somerset family.

5 LINES OF MYSTICAL FORCE

> 'From ancient hill and stone and steeple
> Guiding path for ancient people,
> Rivers running underground –
> I can almost hear their sound'
>
> Harpers Tate, Lines to a Ley Hunter, date unknown.

THE OLD STRAIGHT TRACK

Born in 1855, Alfred Watkins was the son of a Herefordshire brewer, and travelled widely around the British countryside in the course of working for his father as a representative. Early on in life, whilst experimenting in mind reading and predictions, he realised that he was psychic, but as any such involvement with the occult, in those days, was utterly taboo, he deemed it wiser to repress it.

However, on 20 June 1921, as he stopped on a hill top in Blackwardine, Hertfordshire, to check his map before moving on, Watkins suddenly perceived something that had lain hidden since the days of early man, as if the 50-year self-imposed suppression of his valuable psychic gift was being compensated for in one all-seeing moment of truth.

As he stared in disbelief, the earthy layers accumulated through thousands of years of Man's evolution faded away, and he saw beneath the surface of the landscape a tapestry of straight lines linking hill tops, churches, moats, crossroads, ancient stones, and many other old sites, and knew in that instant that these alignments were by design and not coincidence.

He selected the Saxon word 'ley', meaning 'lea' or a tract of open ground, to describe his discovery of these ancient trackways, the existence of which he devoted the remainder of his life to proving.

It was not an easy task for his whole ley concept was derided by the scientific demagogues of the day. And yet Watkins had his admirers, for he was as straight in all his dealings as the undeviating tracks which his psychic perception had revealed, and these admirers formed a Postal Club named after his book *The Old Straight Track* which was published in 1925, the purpose of the club being to link nationally those persons interested in seeking out and discovering leys for themselves. In fact, ley-hunting expeditions were organised, usually with picnics *en route*, becoming a popular pastime in the early 1930s during which time the club flourished and interest in Watkins's ley concept greatly increased.

Watkins himself was much liked and respected by all who knew him. A keen photographer, he had invented several pieces of photographic equipment, notably the Watkins exposure meter which was produced in Hereford. Here, also, in the City Museum are housed the entire collection of his photographs, many of which depict visually for the first time the existence of the ley system.

Prior to publication of *The Old Straight Track*, Watkins had published *Early British Trackways* in 1922, being followed in 1927 by *The Ley Hunters' Manual* and *The Archaic Tracks around Cambridge* in 1932. Although he pondered over some of the alignments of the leys, believing them to have an astronomical significance, his ever-present fear of public ridicule kept him from delving further into their undoubted occult connection. However, he found himself attracted more and more by the spiritual and religious aspect of leys, and discovered many relevant passages in the Bible which he felt confirmed a type of mystical ideology that stretched back beyond the days of the Old Testament.

He was, however, essentially a practical man, and in tracking ley lines, devised a points system whereby churches (which he theorised were built on old pagan sites), beacons and castles, etc. he made 'ley markers', and in order to basically evaluate his system, if the points awarded for each alignment added up to five, then the ley was valid.

He impressed the need for flexibility in ley hunting, maintaining that his own points system should not be dogmatically adhered to as many of the leys he had discovered failed to add up to five – which only goes to show the man's inherent honesty – and prompted Major F.C. Tyler, secretary of the Old Straight Track Club to comment: 'The discovery of new alignments is as much by feel as accurate map work. The ancient races were not obliged to follow a marking system.' Nevertheless, students of Watkins continued to use the system he prescribed, as set out below.

Mounds (1 point)
Usually referred to as tumuli, they are often burial sites dating from the Stone Age. The oldest type of mound is the Neolithic long barrow, which was used for burials and is usually unchambered. Megalithic tombs, however, do contain some form of stone passage or chamber, and modern researchers have discovered evidence indicating that ceremonies and rituals took place within them.

Old Stones (1 point)
Standing Stones,which are prehistoric and can be found in fields or hedgerows and open areas of landscape, are fairly large. Markstones are, however, slightly different, being smaller and dumpy in appearance and tend to be associated with old rural areas. Stone circles have been the objects of much discussion for many years as their history and reason for existence still remains much of a mystery. Years of stringent research on the part of Professor Alexander Thom has, however, gone at least part of the way to proving Watkins's theories.

Water Markers (1 point)
Often referred to as circular moats, they are sometimes found as ditches around tumuli.

Castles (1 point)
These are often sites which have evolved from earlier structures. Watkins believed that Norman castles were built on prehistoric mounds, which the Normans then enlarged by digging earth up from their defensive trench.

Beacons (1 point)
A year after publication of his book *Early British Trackways*,

Watkins realised that beacons aligned on leys, and he also discovered that hills which incorporated the word 'tan', such as St Anne, Beltane, were ancient beacon sites. Names like 'cole', 'black' and 'midsummer' were also similarly connected.

Traditional Wells (1 point)
These include holy wells which were sunk into churchyards and cathedral sites such as that at Winchester.

Churches (¾ – 1 point)
There is now strong evidence to suggest that churches were built on old pagan sites (as dealt with in greater detail after this section) and Watkins quotes from Johnson's *Byways in British Archaeology*: 'It is on record that Patrick, bishop of the Hebrides, desired Orlygus to build a church wherever he found upright stones or menhirs.' Nowadays, most modern ley hunters would consider churches as major ley points worthy of being awarded 1 point in the evaluation system.

Crossroads (¾ point)
Roman and Celtic folklore tell us that events that have occurred at crossroads have been iniquitous and surrounded by intrigue. Murderers, criminals and suicides were traditionally buried there, and crossroads were especially feared after dark when they were said to be haunted by the devil and ghosts of the dead. They were, of course, one of Hecate's favourite places. Watkins's viewpoint was that only ancient track crossings in the countryside or at road junctions bearing ancient names should be considered as valid ley points.

Camps (½ point)
These are often referred to as hill-forts.

There are other, lesser, ley points incorporating the Watkins system, but for the purposes of this investigation it is not necessary to list them.

With regard to churches being built on old pagan sites, there is ample evidence to corroborate this belief although at first sight it seems unlikely that new Christian churches should be deliberately erected on such sites. However, the reigning Pope in a letter to the Christian authorities in England, advised them to do this, being of the opinion that people would go to the ancient sacred sites anyway and that it would be wiser to adapt in this way rather than have the new Christian church make itself unpopular by the destruction of the sites of ancient worship and ritual. 'The English Nation, placed in an obscure corner of the world, has hitherto been wholly taken up with the adoration of wood and stones', wrote Pope Gregory to the Bishop of Alexandria, and according to the laws of Knut, the chief objects of Anglo-Saxon worship were 'the sun and the moon, fire and water, springs, stones and trees', it being the object of the Christian church to convert the followers of these natural forces as soon as their obstinacy would allow.

From the many edicts issued by the Church between AD 500 and 1100, this was apparently quite a lengthy procedure, for the magical practices and pagan rituals exerted a strong power over the people. Consequently, Church leaders were forced to take stronger action, and among the things rigidly banned were:

(1) Idolatry and worship of demons
(2) Cult of the dead
(3) Worship of nature such as trees, wells, stones, fire, etc.
(4) Pagan calendar customs and festivals
(5) Witchcraft and sorcery
(6) Augury and divination and
(7) Astrology.

No one was permitted to visit trees, or wells or stones, or circles, or go anywhere except to God's church. St Eligius, bishop of Noyon, enlarged on this edict in about AD 640 when he said:

'Let no Christian place lights at the temples, or the stones, or at fountains, or at trees, or enclosures, or at places where three ways meet ... let no-one presume to make lustrations (purification by sacrifice) or to enchant herbs, or to make flocks pass through a hollow tree or an aperture in the earth; for by doing so he seems to consecrate them to the devil.'

'The practices were extraordinarily persistent,' Francis Hitching goes on to say in his book *Earth Magic*. During the reign of King Edgar (959–975) the clergy were told that they must 'totally extinguish every heathenism; and forbid well-worshipping and necromancies, and divinations ... with various trees and stones' and that 'any woman who would cure her infant by any sorcery, or shall have it drawn through the earth at the crossroads, is to fast for three years, for this is great paganism'. In 1035, King Knut forbade the barbarous 'worship of stones, trees, fountains and the heavenly bodies'.

The instruction which dominated the attitude of the Christian Church to the old religion was contained in a letter from Pope Gregory to St Augustine, telling him

'by no means to destroy the temples of the idols belonging to the English, but only the idols which are found in them; let holy water be sprinkled over them, let altars be constructed, and relics placed in them, inasmuch as these temples are well constructed it is necessary that they should be converted from the dowership of demons to the true God'.

Mr Hitching continues:

'Thus it was that in countless churches ... the power of the ancient megaliths was assimilated and consecrated by the Christian missionaries. The sites chosen – circles, dolmens, holy trees, wells – had stood untouched for thousands of years, the continuing centres of ceremonies ... retaining through the years some of their original power and force. (This unbroken tradition of worship helps answer one of the principal archaeological objections to Alfred Watkins's definition of points that can be counted in a ley line: that it covers sites of widely differing eras – Stone Age, Bronze Age, Iron Age, Roman and Anglo-Saxon). All the evidence is that the centres were not, as they have so often been interpreted, merely isolated burial chambers or casually placed memorial stones, but a network so constructed that each monument could be used as the focal centre of local custom and magic.'

The more Watkins and his associates researched into the enigma of leys, the more they became convinced that they were not just traveller's tracks laid out as a network but that something far greater lay behind them, for it was as if some sort of current was flowing along these ancient pathways – unseen, mysterious, but wholly powerful.

The behaviour of birds, bees and other animals in relation to their pattern of travel and migration along certain lines, were all noted by members of the Straight Track Club, and realisation that some other force was at work within the ley phenomenon quickly grew, but here again it was Watkins's fear of any involvement with the occult which prevented him from delving deeper into this fascinating problem. In *The Old Straight Track* he concluded by saying:

'I feel that ley-men, astonomer-priest, druid, bard, wizard, witch, palmer and hermit were all more or less linked by one thread of ancient knowledge and power, however degenerate it became in the end.'

When Watkins died on the 5 April 1935, Major Tyler continued researching into ley power, although unhappily he only survived Watkins by about four years.

Tyler, however, re-examined the physical evidence for leys and became convinced that they formed part of a huge geometrical pattern laid down primarily for religious purposes by an ancient people who nevertheless had an unsurpassed knowledge of nature. He was very interested in Dr Josef Heinsch's paper written in 1939 and entitled *Principles of Prehistoric Cult Geography* in which the German geographer expounded his belief of some lost magic principle by which sites of holy centres had been located in the dim past and which he thought were placed on geometric lines constructed in relation to the positions of the heavenly bodies. By its accuracy of construction, Dr Heinsch believed that this vast astronomical and geometrical network, which existed throughout Europe and the Near East, provided evidence of a past civilization with advanced knowledge of science and magic. He further postulated that by means of a force activated through sacred centres on correctly placed geographically-related lines, human beings could be greatly benefited. Thus was Watkins's conviction that leys were far more than just traders' pathways independently confirmed.

With the deaths of both Watkins and Tyler and the outbreak of World War 2, all thoughts of investigating ley power further were shelved, and with only a token interest being maintained in the Straight Track Club, it was eventually disbanded in 1948.

COILS OF SERPENT POWER

Guy Underwood, an archaeologist and dowser, was from a later generation than Watkins and spent much of his time during the 1950s and 1960s researching the earth force mystery. Like Watkins and his club members earlier, Underwood felt that migratory birds were guided by their sense of this earth current, and although he did not openly support Watkins's theories, in his own pursuance of them discovered that all prehistoric geographical alignments coincided with centres and lines of a subterranean nature. Stone circles and their centres together with other points where lines converged were sources of high energy, and Underwood named them 'blind springs'. These, he discovered, were primary power outlets transmitted by the ancient stone uprights. In his book *The Pattern of the Past*, posthumously published in 1969, he wrote:

'... the three geodetic lines – the water line, the aquastat and the track line – appear to have much in common; they appear to be generated within the earth; to involve wave motion; to have great penetrative power; to form a network on the face of the earth; to affect the manner of growth and germination of certain trees and plants; to be perceived and used by animals; to affect opposite sides of the animal body and to form spiral patterns.'

Underwood also found that churches were sited and built on lines of magnetic current, the strongest spring of which is often located directly underneath the tower where the terrestrial force combines with the more divine influences assumed to be attracted by the spire. In fact, the entire geographical arrangement of Britain's prehistoric buildings and other works all coincided, he discovered, with the lines and centres of such subterranean influence. Standing stones mark the paths and spirals of underground streams, cracks and other features associated with intensified magnetism, the centre of every stone circle being a particularly strong source of energy. The current that runs along these three types of geodetic lines is related everywhere to ancient engineering and, according to Underwood, the direction of its flow varies with the phases of the moon.

After Underwood's death in 1964 at the age of 81, retired electrical engineer Bill Lewis, who, like Underwood, was a respected dowser, continued where the older man left off. A strong supporter of Underwood's theories, Lewis also found that there was an intersection of underground streams beneath each active standing stone, and through his knowledge of electrical engineering, realised that the movement of water through a tunnel of earth creates a small static electric field. This field becomes even stronger where the subterranean streams cross, and the standing stone situated immediately above this point acts as a form of amplifier, with the power ascending from the ground and winding around it. As it emerged from below ground, this power became perspicuous in the form of a seven-coiled spiral with the two lower rings, Lewis claimed, being underground. But, unlike Underwood had before him, Lewis found this force to be unstable, apparently decreasing and increasing in cycles according to the phases of the moon or other planetary influences. He discovered, also, that it changed polarity about once a month, becoming disorientated for a short time – a matter of hours or days – before reappearing in a spiral ascending in the opposite direction, standing stones which had become damaged in some way being far less active in this respect.

Tom Graves, another dowser, took Lewis's discoveries a stage further when he found that a power current existed which travelled between the standing stones. He also noted a similar charge flow at other sites and earthworks, and that this charge travelled above ground in straight lines similar to Watkins's straight tracks. Graves called his lines 'overgrounds', and discovered that their intensity altered with the waxing and waning of the moon. As with all such painstaking discoveries, however, scientific proof was badly needed. Fortunately, it was forthcoming.

While author Francis Hitching was working with Bill Lewis on his television documentary and book *Earth Magic*, prompted by Lewis he invited two scientists to test Lewis's theory concerning power spirals at standing stones. Accordingly, Professor John Taylor of King's College, London, and Argentinian physicist Dr Eduardo Balanovski from Imperial College, London, made tests on the 12-foot high standing stone near Crickhowell in South Wales which Lewis claimed emitted a force but which he could not prove.

By using a gaussmeter, which measures static magnetic field strength, Balanovski confirmed that a large charge of electromagnetic activity occurred at the standing stone, and when at Taylor's request Lewis made chalk marks on the stone where he maintained the energy ascended in the form of a coil, the gaussmeter showed twice the strength on many of these marked bands than it recorded on the rest of the standing stone, with all the bands giving a positive reaction on the machine.

The result surprised Balanovski, who declared that in his opinion, the stone had not been accidentally placed there, adding, 'The people who put it there knew about its power, even if they didn't know about electro-magnetism.'

Since 1977, Dr Don Robins of the University of London had headed a team of researchers investigating, amongst other stone circles, the Rollright Stones in Oxfordshire. Using ultrasonic equipment they were able to detect surges of power occurring at the same time as the astronomical equinoxes and solstices. Infrared photographs of the King Stone Rollright monolith, taken at dawn, revealed a subtle emanation of light radiating from the stone's top, and in 1982 Dr Robins reported that after carrying out extensive tests on the site, anomalies in the level of background radiation had been recorded. In his opinion this was proof that the energy flowing between sacred sites was no myth, and he believed that with further scientific study its existence would be proved beyond all doubt.

Following the publication in the *New Scientist* of Dr Robins' findings, the independent scientific tests carried out by a retired BBC engineer at the Rollright stone circle were also made known. He had discovered, through fluctuations in the local magnetic field, that several ley lines converged at the centre of the circle, their existence being confirmed by a dowser who was present on the site at the time. The engineer also discovered that the magnetic pattern inside the circle of standing stones formed a seven-ring spiral similar to those recorded by both Lewis and Graves. How ironic that 60 years after Alfred Watkins had discovered leys, successors of the scientific establishment that had so ridiculed his work should find themselves on the verge now of being able to officially confirm his theories.

LEGACY OF THE DODMEN

This was the name given by Watkins to those prehistoric surveyors who plotted the ancient leys, a name which, he said, after much thought on the subject 'came to him in a flash'. The word 'dod' figures largely in ancient place-names throughout Britain, the meaning varying but little in different parts of the country. In the North of England the term means a 'rounded eminence' whilst in the South it applies to the mound of a castle keep, Dodman's Point being a clifftop castle in Cornwall. The prehistoric outline cut into the chalk on the steep slope of Wilmington Hill in Sussex depicting a man carrying a long pole in each hand, is thought to be an ancient illustration of a dodman or prehistoric surveyor, the poles being used as the 'sighting rods' so essential in his work. These staves, or wands, were an emblem of his authority as well as being, it is thought, a symbol of supernatural power.

The harmonious siting of sacred buildings together with a network of magical pathways planned to locate them is known the world over, although the existence of the Chinese geomancers who practise this science called *feng-shui* (that which cannot be seen or grasped) did not become known in the West until about a hundred years ago; and then only through the complaints of European business-men in China who were being constantly thwarted in their endeavours to site factories, railways and other constructions in certain places by being told by the geomancers that a particular range of hills was a terrestrial dragon, and no cutting could be made through its tail. Therefore alternative routes for proposed railways would have to be found as no tunnels could be made through dragon hills, dragon power being sacred to the Chinese who believed it was a magnetic force which flowed along all *lung-mei* or dragon paths.

Chinese geomancy, which combines science and astrology with an instinctive extra-sensory perception or psychic awareness, has its roots in the Tao philosophy, which in itself can be traced back to 2800 BC. The geomancers connected the flows of earth energy with the symbolic sinuousness of the serpent or dragon, and in this country the druids, too, revered the serpent-dragon as the symbol of force and fertility. As we have noted, with the coming of Christianity all worship of such mysterious earth powers was forbidden, but there is evidence that the builders of medieval churches and cathedrals and members of secret societies such as the Freemasons were able to preserve some of the mystical lore relating to serpent-dragon paths or leys.

One case in point is Chartres Cathedral where a sacred well

was discovered with the statue of a goddess nearby. This was revealed when Christians first visited Chartres, and although they immediately renamed the goddess 'The Black Virgin', pilgrims still travelled from all parts of France to worship and seek cures from her. It is believed that the masons who worked on the building of the cathedral knew about the earth currents and aligned it so as to take full advantage of the abundant psychic power in the area. It is also believed that the druid priests of Chartres had inherited the secret wisdom of serpent power and that at those places where it was most active they were able to tap into this natural power source through the specific placement of the standing stones.

Although the skills of the Chinese geomancers were not widely known outside China, those who travelled were familiar with their esoteric beliefs, such a one being Rudyard Kipling who, when he first visited Batemans, which was to be his home near Burwash in Sussex, is quoted as saying of the seventeenth century house: 'We entered and found her spirit – her *feng shui* – to be good.'

Thus the legacy of the Dodmen lives on, and in *Puck of Pooks Hill* Kipling seems to have appropriately perpetuated its memory:

'Trackway and Camp and City lost,
Salt Marsh where now is corn;
Old Wars, old Peace, old Arts that cease,
And so was England born.'

It is to be hoped that the generations to come will have more of an ecological background and a desire to revive the 'old ways' than had their immediate predecessors.

THE GAIAN HYPOTHESIS

Writing in 1981 of 'Spiritual Patterns', Michael Howard tells of a conference in Princeton, New Jersey, which took place in 1969 when Professor James Lovelock, a Fellow of the Royal Society and consultant to the NASA space programme, put forward the hypothesis that the whole range of life on earth – from algae to oaks, bacteria to whales – is a vast living organism capable of manipulating the environment to sustain its existence.

Professor Lovelock called this entity *'Gaia'* after the Greek goddess whose name is related to the modern sciences of geography, geophysics and geology, and although at the time his ideas shocked many scientists, others who studied his comprehensive evidence came to share his belief that our planet is a living, intelligent entity which can best be described as 'the Earth Spirit'.

This, of course, has long been believed by the ancient peoples living in their tribal lands and worshipping at their secret places, who identified with an Earth Mother with whom they lived in harmony by observing all the natural rhythms. Their whole life-style was built around their belief that the earth was a living organism infused with a spirit which they naturally respected and nurtured.

Modern ley hunters acknowledge this too in that they realise that alignments between sites are like a psychic power grid with its mesh of subterranean forces and straight overground energy paths linking with cosmic and atmospheric influences, the whole combining together to make up the living spirit of the earth, and they, like today's ecologists and other deep-thinking people, utterly abhor the desecration of this sacred life force, this rape of *Gaia*.

To Guy Underwood it was a dismal fact that there existed certain 'dead' areas in the countryside where there was a marked absence of plant and animal life, similar to that commented upon by visitors to Clapham Wood, and he attributed this unnatural stagnation to the blocking of a ley by, say, the sinking of a mineshaft or construction of foundations for new buildings which interfered with the natural earth current. This blockage was subsequently called by ley-men a 'black stream', and not only did it poison the atmosphere but could even cause physical sickness to those living in the immediate area.

The Chinese geomancers, however, as previously mentioned, took great care that this did not happen, for they knew that the life force of the dragon paths could be corrupted and soured by irresponsible man-made constructions and that if the dragon's tail, for instance, became blocked or cut in this way, the life force could not flow, leading thus to its mortification like a human limb deprived of blood and becoming gangrenous. Where this had, however, unfortunately occurred, they believed that the corrupted force could be manipulated by any evil sorcerers for their own ends and used to the detriment of others.

Clapham is the connecting point for leys coming from Chanctonbury Ring and Cissbury Ring, with both of which it forms a triangle. Some of these leys are blocked by man-made obstructions and must therefore be classified as 'black streams'. This concentration of soured ley power is a veritable hot-bed of toxicity, making Clapham an ideal centre for any who wish (and have the knowledge) to tap the supply for malefic purposes. Is this what the Friends of Hecate are doing?

6 CHANCTONBURY AND CISSBURY – RINGS OF ENERGY IN THE RAPE OF BRAMBER

'The past lives on with the concrete present, nothing destroyed, the layered centuries preserve all, everything exists for ever, out of sight and sound, waiting to be lifted into the light.'

Leonard Clark

CHANCTONBURY RING

This aloof and lovely lord of the southern hills is the most noted landmark in Sussex. It was said that sailors marked it from their ships in the Channel, and motorists travelling south could see it in the blue distance as soon as they had breasted the Surrey hills. A famous beauty spot, it can be seen clearly from almost any point on the ridge of the South Downs.

Rising some 780 feet above sea level, it is crowned with a ring of beech trees which make a conspicuous and beautiful circle on the hill's bold bluff. They were planted in 1760 by Charles Goring in whose large estate Chanclebury, as it was then called, was situate. As a boy, Charles looked up at the bare top and in his mind's eye 'saw it dressed with a grove of trees', whereupon he immediately made up his mind to plant them.

'With what delight I placed those twigs,' he afterwards wrote, and so that they should strike root he carried water daily, for months, up to the hill to them, at that time writing, in verse, that he had

'...an almost hopeless wish that would creep within my breast,
Oh! could I live to see thy top in all its beauty dressed!'

He got his wish for he lived to be a very old man and saw his young trees established and thriving. In 1828 he recorded his love of the Ring in a poem:

Chanclebury Ring

Say what you will, there is not in the world
A nobler sight than from this upper Down.
No rugged landscape here, no beauty hurled
From its Creator's hand as with a frown;
But a green plain on which green hills look down
Trim as a garden plot. No other hue
Can hence be seen, save here and there the brown
Of a square fallow, and the horizon's blue.
Dear checker-work of woods, the Sussex Weald.
If a name thrills one yet of things of earth,
That name is thine. How often I have fled
To thy deep hedgerows and embraced each field,
Each lag, each pasture, – fields which gave me birth
And saw my youth, and which must hold me dead.

Charles Goring of Wiston

Although it is thought by many that Chanctonbury was named after the ring of trees, the ring was there well before the trees were planted for it derives its name from the circular earthwork made by the early Celts over 2000 years before. Excavations carried out this century have revealed that the ramparts of the hill-fort date from about 300 BC and the several pits that were found, thought at first to be the remains of prehistoric dwellings, were in fact mine shafts driven into the chalk about 2500 BC. The Ring consists of the ancient fort's ditch and rampart which form an oval enclosure with diameters of about 550 feet by 400 feet. It has two entrances, one on the east and the other on the western part of the rampart, and where the ground slopes away the defensive works are powerfully developed whilst on the north-west side where it skirts the steep escarpment of the hill the earthwork is comparatively slight.

The early Celts erected such hill-forts in all commanding positions of the Downs, and with nearby Cissbury Ring and Rackham, Chanctonbury Ring forms the 'Devil's Triangle', for legend has it that the devil had a hand in the formation of these three downland hills when he discovered that the inhabitants of Sussex were being converted from paganism to Christianity. Consequently he decided to drown them all, and began digging a gigantic trench down to the sea from Poynings (Devil's Dyke) sending large quantities of earth in every direction. One pile became Chanctonbury, another Cissbury and the third Rackham.

Those who came after the original builders of the Chanctonbury hill-fort developed the site still more, especially the Romans, who built a sunken temple and surrounded it with a court in a Romano-Celtic style peculiar to Southern England and France north of Provence and west of the Rhine. Being partly underground, it may have been a temple to Mithra, an Iranian deity whose original worship in Persia was held in caves, and which was introduced to the Romans in 68 BC, although I have not heard this postulated before. However, Mithraism was very popular with the Roman legions over here. This worship of the God of Light (which, incidentally, was early Christianity's most formidable rival) entailed secret ceremonies and rituals from which all women were excluded, and which were conducted amid much mystery in underground caves or specially built subterranean chambers.

Many coins have been found at this ancient shrine, from those made in the time of Nero (AD 54–68) to Gratian (AD 375–83). Other coins belonging to Tetricus the Elder have also been uncovered, but these were minted in Britain after the Romans left. This Roman temple must have been in use some 300 years or more by the Romans, for hundreds of little coloured stones – *tesserae* of which they made their well-known pavements – were dug up there in 1908. There was also evidence that an ancient tile-maker worked there, and the imprint of an animal's foot – probably his dog or other pet – was found on a tile, obviously having been made by the creature before the tile was fired.

In 1977 a team led by archaeologist Dr Owen Bedwin carried out a dig at the Ring prior to the replanting of trees, and he did not think there had been a Roman occupation of the Ring although he thought the temple and shrine uncovered in 1909 had been used by people visiting the site for rituals, though what form such rituals might have taken wasn't known.

There was a large dew pond at Chanctonbury which never dried up and became as well-known as the clump of trees from 1874 onwards, but during World War 2, when Chanctonbury was used for army exercises involving tanks and armoured cars, etc., these vehicles left their mark, the dew pond disappeared, and only a slight declivity in the turf marks the spot now. The Long Furlong dew pond at Clapham also dried up after World War 2.

But despite all such desecration, Chanctonbury's inherent magic remains, as if sustained by an occult reservoir, and it is probably the magnetic presence of this unseen force which creates its air of mystery and propagates so many unexplained phenomena within the Ring.

ENCHANTED ATMOSPHERE

Stillness and silence are peculiar to beechwoods as only about one-fifth of sunlight reaches the ground, which is often thickly carpeted with fallen leaves, and the remaining four-fifths are shaded and lifeless and, for most of the year, dark and consequently eerie. However, there is much more than this characteristic atmosphere at Chanctonbury where, inside the Ring, no birds sing and the place seems bereft of even the smallest woodland creature, which, as Charles Walker comments, gives you a very uneasy feeling. He says:

'Suddenly you realise you are alone, with nothing but the trees – some of which are dead or dying – and yet you feel you're being watched, followed, and the chill that comes upon you as you enter the Ring increases with every step you take. Although the area covered by the trees is not large and they are by no means densely packed, walking from one end to the other seems to take forever, and gives you a feeling of utter isolation.'

Such an atmosphere is naturally conducive to witchcraft, with which Chanctonbury has long been associated, together with hauntings, unseen forces and, in more modern times, with UFO sightings.

Evidence of practitioners of the black arts was found by Charles Walker in 1979 inside the Ring in the form of the remains of a black altar which he photographed, and in 1982 I photographed a group of pointed tree stumps each about 8 feet high, which suddenly appeared on a plateau outside the Ring at a point where two ley lines pass through from Clapham. One ley emanates from Clapham church and the other passes through the crossroads site in Clapham Wood where many leys converge. The tree stumps were arranged in a circle, and were there for only a matter of weeks, after which they disappeared as mysteriously as they had appeared.

Among those said to haunt the Ring are a Saxon shade, a midnight druid and a royal Carian ghost.

The white-bearded Saxon, said to have been killed at Hastings, was often seen wandering about Chanctonbury looking for his lost treasure, so the story went, for he was often in a crouching position scrabbling amongst the leaves as if searching for something buried, until 1866 when late that year a ploughman turned up a valuable hoard of Anglo-Saxon silver coins in a crock under the hill. The Saxon shade was not seen anywhere on Chanctonbury after this.

If you walk round the Ring twelve times at midnight on Midsummer Night, and presumably only then, it is said the midnight druid will come over the earthwork to you, and in the dimness of the Ring's interior on such a magical night this would not be difficult to imagine. Druids were, of course, associated with Chanctonbury as with many other Celtic hill-forts, which they fortified, for it was they who organised the opposition to the Roman invasion of 55–54 BC when Julius Caesar was forced to retreat.

The druidic religion, based on fertility cults which entailed many cruel ceremonies including human sacrifice, which were always carried out in a grove of sacred oak trees, became firmly established in about 350 BC, and in their capacity as priest-kings, the druids brought about an overall cohesion of the warring Celtic tribes. Under their specialised instruction, the beginnings of a fighting army and warrior class of Celt emerged. The priesthood was eventually overcome by the Roman general Suetonius Paulinus in their last druidic stronghold on the island of Anglesey in AD 58. However, the druidic cult, with its unequalled knowledge of Nature's powers, lingers on in many Celtic parts of the country today, its dubious ceremonial worship still being conducted on ancient sites in oak groves (or their equivalent) in the utmost secrecy, one known site being historic Primrose Hill in London.

The third spectre said to haunt Chanctonbury is the royal Carian ghost. In the early days of the seventeenth century,

Prince Agasicles Syenness, an astrologer from Caria (where, incidentally, the goddess Hecate is purported to have originated), seems to have taken up permanent residence at the Ring in order to study the stars. Very little is known about him beyond the fact that, according to a Sussex writer, 'he had no sense of breeches' (a saying which applied to underlings when they unwisely attempted to go beyond their station in life), but several people have reported a feeling of coldness inside the Ring which heralds the sudden appearance of a tall misty shape gliding in and out of the trees. No-one has apparently remained long enough to investigate the apparition more closely.

The Ring's mysterious atmosphere has also been commented upon by author Dr Philip Gosse who lived at Wiston where he could see the Ring from his bedroom window, much to his joy, for, like Charles Goring, he loved Chanctonbury. In an interview in 1935 he said:

'Naturally the Ring is haunted. Even on bright summer days there is an uncanny sense of some unseen presence which seems to follow you about. If you enter the dark wood alone you are conscious of something behind you. When you stop, it stops. When you go on, it follows. Even on the most tranquil days when no breath of air stirs the leaves, you can hear a whispering somewhere above you, and if you should be so bold as to enter the Ring on a dark night, as my wife and I did ...'

He didn't go into detail, merely shuddered and ended,

'We never shall repeat that visit; some things are best forgotten if they can be, and certainly not set down in a book.'

Obviously, Dr and Mrs Gosse experienced something strange and frightening, as have many others who have been far less reticent in recounting what happened, although a group of University students who planned to spend the night at the Ring to take tape recordings and photographs, left in a panic-stricken rush, leaving all their equipment behind, when they were 'frightened out of their wits' by a supernatural incident in 1967. No amount of cajoling from reporters afterwards could tempt any of them to recount what actually happened, and, like Dr and Mrs Gosse thirty years previously, they would only vow that never again would they repeat their night-time visit to Chanctonbury Ring.

On Saturday, 15 June 1968, an all-night vigil was held at the Ring by a UFO research group by the name of the Sussex Sky-watchers. During the early hours of Saturday morning, one of their members was walking about inside the clump of trees when he suddenly lost the use of his limbs, and fell to the ground shouting to the others for help. When they rushed to his aid they, too, found themselves similarly affected, and although the paralysis was only temporary, they were all acutely aware of an unseen presence which made their feeling of helplessness even more frightening.

Also in June 1968, a UFO watch consisting of a group of eight men and one woman was organised by writer John Killick, who chose Chanctonbury simply because it was the highest point and the one most convenient to reach from their homes in Brighton, Southwick and Worthing. When they entered the Ring, they had not gone far before they experienced a remarkable drop in temperature. Mr Killick said that waves of coldness swamped them, affecting their feet first, and causing some members of the group to have stomach cramps, others to feel ill, and one to experience difficulty in breathing. They hurriedly left the inside of the trees, and quickly recovered, but all of them were alarmed by the occurrence and the eerie feeling that there was a strange presence observing them at the time. They did not intend repeating their visit.

In October 1972, Mr Simpson of Worthing was walking over Chanctonbury with two friends on an overcast, chilly evening that was nevertheless pleasant for walking. As they approached the enclosure of trees at about 11.00 pm they saw a flickering light inside, and assumed someone had lit a bonfire. However, as they got nearer the light disappeared and the place was deserted and very still and silent. Suddenly as they approached the centre of the Ring a loud swishing noise caused them to gaze upwards and they all three saw a dull red glow coming from a large oblong object which appeared to be brushing the tops of the trees although it made no sound itself.

'We were frozen to the spot', Mr Simpson is reported to have said, 'and could not believe what we were clearly seeing with our own eyes', and as they felt relatively safe whilst under the trees they did not break cover until the object had moved away beyond the clump. They said it appeared to be illuminated by a blue glow, and after hovering for about 30 seconds it shot up into the night sky at a terrific speed. (This object, or one similar, was sighted again in December 1979 by independent witnesses who said it disappeared in the direction of Brighton.)

In the summer of 1974, a brilliant white circular object was seen shooting up the west side of the hill, where it hovered for about 45 seconds before changing its shape to an oblong and disappearing in a north-westerly direction at great speed, and the following summer a bright orange object was seen in the sky over Cissbury Ring. After hovering for a brief few moments it shot off at high speed towards Chanctonbury. Within moments of this sighting, a woman walking her dog at Chanctonbury reported seeing a large round bright orange object land on the west side of Chanctonbury Hill. She said it remained on the ground for no more than a minute, then shot straight up into the air and was lost to sight within seconds.

This seems to be the usual pattern of behaviour as regards UFOs or lights reported in the area, for they are first seen at Cissbury Ring travelling towards Chanctonbury Ring, and then independently reported from the latter area.

Perhaps the most alarming experience of all happened at Chanctonbury Ring on 25 August 1974, when Charles Walker and three other members of the Ghost and Psychic Investigation Group were walking inside the ring of trees. It was about 11.00 pm when one member – William Lincoln – was suddenly levitated by a force that took him some 5 feet into the air, where he hung suspended for about 60 seconds before being 'released' and crashing back to the ground. During this terrifying experience, of which there is a tape recording, he was pleading with the unseen force and crying out 'No more! No more!' and not only was he badly shaken afterwards but his back was hurt when he hit the ground. Needless to say, he vowed never again to visit Chanctonbury and this whole episode was witnessed by the other members of the group, Charles Walker, Dave Wills and Richard Walker.

Five years later, Charles Walker and Dave Wills returned with several other members of the group, which did not, of course, include Mr Lincoln, to make a further investigation, and as they approached the spot where Mr Lincoln had been levitated, Mr Wills was suddenly knocked to the ground by an invisible force whilst another member had a crucifix he was wearing around his neck wrenched off and flung aside. When he retrieved it, not only had the fixing link been twisted and broken, but the article was burning hot to the touch.

It is of course well-known that all sites of ancient temples where mystery rituals have been worked generate a strong psychic force, especially at night, those on leys or with druidic connections being extremely potent. Author John Michell, in his book *The New View Over Atlantis* enlarges on this in his chapter on 'Sacred Engineering' when he writes:

'... It is certain that underground caverns, both natural and artificial, were the scenes of prehistoric magical rites. In several cases their entrances have been found directed onto leys or towards significant astronomical declinations ... The Druids, in common with the shamans of Asia and North America are said to have accomplished magical flights, often from those very mounds and hill-tops where the great heroes of mythology achieved their apotheosis. There may be something about such places which attracts those forces capable of modifying the normal influence of gravity, or which, alternatively, reacts upon an intensified field of human magnetism to produce circumstances conducive to levitation.'

The incidents I have related certainly substantiate Mr Michell's research and views very fully, and an interesting point in connection with the crucifix is that its wearer had once lived at Clapham, and while resident there had had it blessed by the vicar of Clapham church, the Reverend Neil Snelling.

Does not the abuse of this sanctified artefact prove beyond all reasonable doubt that a druidic or other occult anti-Christian presence really does haunt mystical Chanctonbury Ring?

But it was not any occult presence that alarmed Charles Walker and Dave Wills when they made one of their periodic night visits to Chanctonbury in the late autumn of 1983, when just before midnight they saw headlights approaching along the A 24 and coming up the steep track of the hill. As the vehicle drew nearer a rotating spotlight was switched on. Intrigued, the two men moved from the cover of the trees to the perimeter of the Ring to take a closer look, for they recognised the vehicle as a landrover and could see from the outline of its occupants that the figures appeared to be holding up long sticks. However, no sooner had they broken cover and were standing watching the landrover than a shot rang out in their direction.

Scarcely able to believe what was happening, the two men promptly turned tail and dashed back into the cover of the trees. As they were doing so, further shots followed them and they heard the sound of pellets hitting the trees and fragmenting the bark just above their heads as they dodged through the maze of beeches with the spotlight panning their desperate escape.

Somehow they managed to keep out of the way of both the searchlight and the bullets until they reached the steep incline at the back of the Ring, down which they scrambled at breakneck speed to safety.

Charles thought at first that he and Dave had been mistaken for deer poachers, however unlikely this was in their unarmed state, but when a similar, though less harrowing, incident occurred some two years later at Clapham, he realised there could be another explanation. On this latter occasion in 1985, Charles was walking at dusk on the public right-of-way through the Chestnuts area of Clapham Wood when he was challenged by a man carrying a broken shot-gun who advised him to turn back, and Charles took an alternative route. Later that evening, as he was coming back through the church-yard path, a spotlight at the side of the Manor House just south of the church was suddenly switched on, illuminating the whole area, and he was again stopped and questioned by another man carrying a shot-gun, who nevertheless allowed him to proceed when he explained he was going back home after taking a walk.

As both places where Charles was challenged were in the vicinity of the sites the Friends of Hecate are known to have used for their meetings, he was reminded of the initiate's warning: *We will stop at nothing to ensure the safety of our cult*, and whilst it is accepted that gamekeepers must be armed in order to protect their stock from poachers, could they not also serve an ulterior purpose?

In retrospect, Charles wondered if the Chanctonbury shooting might not also have indicated the presence of a secret cult – not necessarily the same one that is known to practise at Clapham, but one equally anxious to preserve its secrecy – although the posting of armed sentries in public places and along public pathways seems to be an extreme method to adopt for preserving their security.

CISSBURY RING

Although, at 602 feet above sea level, this hill-fort is not as high as Chanctonbury, nevertheless Cissbury Ring is a notable landmark overlooking Worthing, and lies some three and a half miles from the sea.

Three chalk ridges meet on this distinctive tree-crowned hill, one sloping south towards the sea being called Mount Carvey, the other two ridges being Tenants Hill and Lychpole Hill which both slope south-eastwards towards Sompting. On the north side Cissbury is precipitous as is common along the South Downs, and not only does it command extensive views of the coast from Beachy Head to the Isle of Wight, but the spire of Chichester Cathedral can also be seen from its ancient top.

And ancient Cissbury is, for Neolithic flint miners worked there between 3000 BC and 2000 BC, these mines being amongst the most famous of their kind in Britain. There are in fact several mines which consist of vertical shafts and horizontal galleries, and they can be seen as a hummocky area of pits and mounds in the west part of the hill-fort. They were excavated in the last century and again in the 1950s, antler picks found there giving a carbon date of 2700 BC.

Most of the visible remains of the hill-fort, which ranks in fame and size second only to the famous one at Maiden Castle in Dorset, belong to the Iron Age and were constructed about 250 BC, Cissbury's earthworks occupying an area of some 82 acres in all. The defences consist of a massive rampart and ditch with a smaller counterscarp bank on the outer lip, the original entrances being on the south and east.

It is thought that this important hill-fort was probably used as a tribal stronghold where people took refuge when danger threatened, and into which cattle could be driven, and by virtue of its unique position Cissbury could have served as the headquarters of an area bounded by the River Arun on the west and the River Adur on the east.

During Roman times, farming communities settled there, ploughing and cultivating all the land where it was not occupied by flint-mine shafts, and in Saxon times during the reigns of Aethelred II (AD 1009–16) and Cnut (AD 1017–23) there was a Cissbury Mint, but although many hopeful people have searched for this over the years, the site of the mint has not yet been discovered.

There are plenty of legends connected with its whereabouts, however, the one current in the 1860s telling of a blocked-up tunnel running underground from Offington Hall to Cissbury Ring (a distance of over two miles) which contained 'unimaginable treasure'. The owner of the Hall offered half the money to anyone who would clear this subterranean passage, and although many persons tried and began digging, they were all driven back by 'large and fearsome supernatural snakes' springing at them with gaping jaws and angry hisses.

Similar tales have been recounted down the ages in connection with most prehistoric mounds and earthworks: that mysterious tunnels run beneath them; that they contain treasure which cannot be located; that such circles are enchanted, and that they are magical sites where people have strange experiences.

Many ley lines intersect at Cissbury, some coming direct from Clapham, and there appears to be a strong terminus at a tumulus on Mount Carvey near the top of Cissbury Ring at Vineyard Hill, a site of many unexplained phenomena. As mentioned in the previous chapter, the well-known dowser, Guy Underwood, discovered that megalithic sites and earthen structures – even certain ancient churches – stood over what he called 'blind springs' (which, incidentally, Chinese geomancers called *chin-cao* or 'sleeping water') and he had no doubt that the ancient peoples had an affinity for such places and knew the strange powers they generated. Other dowsers detected above-ground energies at old sites, and as Paul Devereux says in his book *Earth Lights*: 'Not only dowsers, but psychics too have stated over the years that prehistoric sites have mysterious forces operating around them'.

Whilst there have been many reports of UFO activity and mysterious lights being seen in the vicinity of Cissbury Ring, most of them have been observed making for nearby Chanctonbury Ring, as previously mentioned, as if some magnetism exists between the two ancient henges. Light 'flashes' have also been seen emanating from the region of Cissbury's top at certain times of the year, as if the energy it generates builds up and has to be released, but whether this has any influence on UFO activity is impossible to say. Paul Devereux found, when researching *The Ley Hunter's Companion*, that 37.5 per cent of the leys they selected showed some evidence of UFO events occurring in them or in their immediate vicinity, and referring to this in *Earth Lights*, Mr Devereux says:

'I think that ancient sites, and therefore leys, tend to occur particularly strongly in areas that attract considerable UFO activity. Although some people make wild claims about the relationship between UFOs and leys, I have not seen any hard evidence to make a more specific statement than that.'

ENERGY SOURCES

The word 'energy' comes from the Greek *energeia* meaning activity, and was coined by Aristotle from the word elements *en-* (in) plus *ergon* (work). Through the occult writings of a group of Alexandrian philosophers a century or so after Aristotle, the concept 'cosmic forces' (from the term *hai energiai*) entered Western thought. The poet Samuel Taylor Coleridge introduced into our language in the nineteenth century the psychological meaning of energy (from *psyche*, breath of life) as being 'vigour or intensity of action', which, together with its later scientific connotations, encapsulated within its meaning spiritual, cosmic and occult forces.

That UFOs, mysterious lights, even ghostly and other nebulous apparitions, are forms of energy bodies that can change their shape, density, direction and speed of flow or flight in accordance with the vagaries of air currents or electromagnetic fields, seems a highly probable concept in regard to all such observed phenomena. Being, it would seem, composed of some kind of static electricity, this transient entity would consequently be attracted to other energy bodies (including the human), such motivation giving it the appearance of possessing directional intelligence or even a degree of free will.

In fact, those who have witnessed the appearance of these luminous, shape-shifting entities – particularly those appearing in areas of disused mine-shafts such as exist at Cissbury – have noted this magnetic quality about them, as if they are attracted by human energy and even capable of responding positively to it. Be that as it may, emanations of this nature must surely indicate the existence of an energy source from which the entity originates. Are Chanctonbury and Cissbury Rings reservoirs of such energy, and if so, are the leys channels for this subtle power?

7 VICTIMS OF THE DARK FORCES?

'Truth will come to light; murder cannot be hid long.'

Shakespeare
The Merchant of Venice, II

'I met Murder in the way –
He had a mask like Castlereagh.'

Percy Bysshe Shelley
The Mask of Anarchy, II

'The wicked in his pride ... sitteth in the lurking places of the village: in the secret places doth he murder the innocent.'

From Psalm 10

'NO OBVIOUS NATURAL CAUSE OF DEATH'

This phraseology, together with similar statements such as 'No signs of violence' and 'No evidence of suicide or drugs', littered newspaper reports of the mysterious deaths which occurred in the Chanctonbury/Wiston area and Clapham Wood between 1972 and 1981. Only in one instance was murder officially designated (that of Mrs Jillian Matthews in 1981), the other bodies being so badly decomposed by the time they were found that much valuable forensic evidence had been lost, thus necessitating open verdicts being returned.

'Extensive decomposition' and 'Cause of death unascertainable' were other unsatisfactory conclusions which cropped up repeatedly in the various reports, causing much grim speculation and leaving unanswered – perhaps for ever – the terrible ultimate question: How did these unfortunate victims really meet their deaths?

Police Constable Peter Goldsmith

PC Goldsmith went missing on Friday, 2 June 1972. He was 46 years of age and lived with his wife, Edith, a State Registered nurse, and their two daughters in Steyning where he was stationed. Earlier that day he had called in at the police station and when he failed to return home later his wife reported him missing. He did not report for early morning shift duty the following morning, and a massive search was then mounted with many police, tracker dogs and a helicopter scouring the nearby South Downs.

By the 20 June, the search was intensified with thirty police and ten police dogs checking every inch of the Downs around Steyning, and on the 22 September a police spokesman disclosed that all enquiries had drawn a blank. 'We have followed up a number of leads but none has proved fruitful,' he said. The extensive search had continued throughout the summer months, using police on horse-back as well as tracker dogs, a helicopter and a sea-diving unit, but no trace of the missing man was found, and his colleagues in the Force as well as his family were utterly baffled, for there was no reason for his disappearance.

Newspaper reports during that summer of 1972 contain discrepancies as to his activities at the time of his disappearance, one saying that he was on a shopping trip whilst another said he had 'gone missing while jogging'. He was well-known in the area, being an imposing figure of 6 feet 6 inches tall and a former Royal Marine Commando. A lover of the countryside, he knew its by-ways well, although Mrs Goldsmith said that when they moved from the Midhurst area to Steyning some two years previously she had not found it easy to settle and had in fact taken a part-time job. Her husband had recently been worrying about his nephew, a police constable at East Grinstead in Sussex, who had been suspended from duty. But on the morning of the 2 June when she last saw her husband, she had reminded him he had to go along to the bank it being Friday, and she had no reason to feel at all apprehensive as she kissed him goodbye as usual.

Six months later on 13 December 1972 his body was found by Mr Edward Llewellyn Harris, a farmer from Fulking who stumbled upon the corpse at 3.00 pm while beating for a shooting party at Pepperscoombe.

At the inquest held on 19 December, Dr Hugh Robert

Johnson, senior lecturer in forensic medicine at St Thomas's Hospital, London, said that PC Goldsmith had obviously lain himself down in a very impenetrable part of the undergrowth within a thick protection of brambles from which it had been necessary to cut a way out in order to remove the body. It was in a position that looked as if the man was asleep on his left side. It was covered with leaves and there was extensive decomposition. It was not as though he had collapsed with a heart attack and it seemed impossible for any other person to have been involved in the death as there was nothing to show a struggle or other form of foul play. The body was well hidden away and could not have been put in that position by anyone else. Death had occurred at least three months or more prior to the discovery of the body, but the cause of death was unaccountable from a pathological point of view.

In PC Goldsmith's left hand was the remains of a disc attached to a metal ring, and beside his body was a bottle half-filled with brown liquid which, after tests, revealed no presence of any poison. The body was also lying on a ley line.

Mr Donald Jones, a civilian clerk at Steyning, confirmed that PC Goldsmith was worried about his nephew and the trouble he was in, and also told the coroner that he seemed to be worried about a sudden death which he had been investigating.

In this connection, Detective Sergeant Ronald Fisher said that PC Goldsmith had been the coroner's officer when the body of a young woman had been found on the Downs in April (1972), ironically only about half a mile from the spot where his own body was eventually discovered. PC John Grigson, who said that he and the dead man had been firm friends, said he had seemed worried recently, was rather quiet and slightly nervous about something. Before his reported disappearance, the two constables had had to destroy some tablets remaining from former inquests at the police station, and as they burnt them, PC Goldsmith is reported to have said, 'All those suicides and sudden deaths come back to me and make me feel sick. I will never do it again.'

Detective Superintendent Charles Tapp, last of the twelve witnesses called, described the immense search which had taken place during which 26 men with dog handlers had been increased to 95 and a helicopter, which went on through July and into August in their vain quest for PC Goldsmith, and the

West Sussex Coroner, Francis Haddock, said that the evidence strongly suggested that PC Goldsmith had killed himself, although medical evidence gave no help except that there was no question of foul play. No-one could exclude the possibility, however remote, that PC Goldsmith had felt unwell and did not intend to kill himself but had taken shelter or something of that sort and died a natural death. He therefore returned an open verdict on the police constable.

Not only did the findings at the inquest pose even more questions, but the wording of some of the statements seem to be a little patronising, if not suspect. For instance, Dr Johnson is reported to have stated that the body could not have been put in the position in which it was found by anyone else, and the coroner, whilst keeping all other options as regards cause of death open, completely discounted any question of foul play. How could they be so sure?

The report of the inquest also stated that PC Goldsmith had obviously lain himself down in a very impenetrable part of the undergrowth beneath thick bramble covered with leaves. Bearing in mind that it was summer at the time of his disappearance and the ground would already have been thick with foliage, would he have gone through all the trouble and discomfort of secreting himself under a thorny bramble patch as well? Even if he had, his clothes must have been ripped or pierced by thorns, but beyond saying that the body was fully clothed when found, no mention of any such tearing seems to have been made. Neither was any mention made of a holdall which he was supposed to have been carrying when last seen.

It was revealed that PC Goldsmith was coroner's officer when the body of a young girl was found just half a mile from the spot where his own body was later to be recovered (which in itself seems to be a remarkable coincidence), and Donald Jones confirmed that the police constable was indeed worried about the girl's sudden death which he had been investigating. He was last seen at 3.30 in the afternoon of Friday, 2 June 1972, carrying a brown canvas holdall and walking in the direction of the Downs above Steyning where her body had been found. Was he, in fact, following up a new lead in connection with the un-named girl's mysterious death? Had he discovered evidence which it would have been healthier for him not to have known? Who was the girl, anyway, and how had she died? No microfilm press reports or details of her death appear to be available now. Why the secrecy?

Had this sensitive and dutiful officer, an athlete well able to look after himself, stumbled upon the truth surrounding her mysterious death, and is this why he, too, had to die? Had he discovered too much? Was there someone – or maybe a group of people – who had too much to lose by his further investigations? What really happened to PC Goldsmith?

Mr Leon Foster

There was no evidence of suicide or crime in the death of Mr Leon Foster whose body was found in Clapham Wood on 4 August 1975, but neither was there any obvious natural cause of death. Sixty-six years of age, Mr Foster loved walking on the Downs, his sister-in-law Mrs Edna Foster said, adding that he had never said he would take his own life. He had been missing for only about three weeks.

Mr Foster's body was found by Mr Hugo Healy and his wife while they were searching for their missing horse which was kept at Long Furlong adjoining Clapham Wood. As they entered the woods Mrs Healy spotted a pair of boots sticking out, and thought it was a tramp asleep, but they reported it to a farmer's wife who called the police. PC Owen Stansmore said that straw had been scattered near the body as if for a bed. 'There were two nylon rain garments and some nylon cord tied to a tree which he could have put the garments on to protect him from the elements,' PC Stansmore added.

Pathologist Dr Ian West said that owing to the state of the body the cause of death was unascertainable but there was only a slight amount of alcohol present in the body and it also appeared that Mr Foster had not eaten or drunk anything for some days prior to death. The combination of these circumstances together with the heat at that time of year could have brought about a natural death, he thought.

In the absence of any 'obvious natural cause of death' due to the rapid decomposition which had taken place and which precluded much valuable forensic evidence, coroner Mr Mark Calvert-Lee returned an open verdict. But what really happened to this harmless, elderly man who loved walking the downland ways? Had he died naturally, or had he, as in Shelley's lines, 'met Murder in the way'?

The Reverend Harry Neil Snelling

'I'll walk home over the Downs,' Father Snelling told his wife when he telephoned her at their Steyning home after keeping a dental appointment at Goring, near Worthing. It was the afternoon of the 31 October 1978, and he was telephoning from a call-box at Findon to ask if she could collect him in the car, but she told him it was still out of action, so he said he would continue walking. He remarked cheerily that the dentist had removed a piece of filling from his gum, and he was in good spirits.

Retired vicar of Clapham and Patching, he was last seen at Findon Park House as he left the A 24 in order to cut across the Downs to Steyning, but was not seen again after this. When he did not arrive home his wife reported him missing, and the following day 25 officers from Steyning, Shoreham, Worthing and Hove, with dog handlers, searched the route the 65-year-old vicar should have taken. He was nowhere to be found. As concern for his safety mounted, a reduced night force of ten police continued the search by torchlight. Then a light aircraft was called in to help and during the days that followed police with tracker dogs as well as civilian helpers combed the Downs for him, but all to no avail.

Later, a Shoreham police spokesman said they were 'continuing all the usual searches with all the available manpower', but as with PC Goldsmith who had disappeared in the same area, all enquiries drew a blank. One year later the position was still the same, with a Shoreham CID officer commenting in an article in the *Worthing Herald* that no information as to the Father Snelling's whereabouts had ever come to light. 'He's still regarded as a missing person and will remain so until something turns up,' he said. In the same article, Mrs Snelling said 'I can only think he collapsed with a heart attack and ended up in some tiny corner of the countryside that's been overlooked. It seems incredible I know.' But every 'tiny corner' of the countryside had been scoured again and again, as it had been in the case of PC Goldsmith, and no vestige of evidence uncovered.

Nearly three years were to pass before his skeletal remains were found, for it was not until August 1981 that a Canadian hiker named Michael Raine, who apparently did not have time to report directly to the police as he was due to fly to Africa the following day, wrote to Worthing police sending them a wallet with Father Snelling's credit card inside, plus a rough sketch showing the woods near Wiston Barn where Mr Raine said the skeleton could be found.

The police search party found the remains 150 yards from the north edge of the woods at Wiston at a place which had been thoroughly searched before. The woods surrounding this area are a Ministry of Defence restricted zone with danger notices displayed to mark the locality. Why Father Snelling should have gone there when all he had to do was keep to the South Downs Way path in order to get home to Steyning is a mystery. Knowing the area as well as he did, how could he possibly have mistaken the path and wandered into the restricted zone, for he would be unlikely to have entered the area deliberately. (And, incidentally, why was Mr Raine supposedly trespassing in the restricted zone when he found the skeletal remains?)

If Father Snelling's body had indeed lain where it was found from the time of his disappearance, surely it would have been so deeply buried in undergrowth, foliage and leaves during the lapse of those three years that finding it at all would seem to have been something of a miracle. Also the fact that the discovery was very conveniently made by a visitor from overseas who was hopping from continent to continent and unable to be questioned in person, only serves to add to the already mounting pile of suspicious circumstances surrounding the death of this kindly old gentleman.

There were similarities between Father Snelling's death and that of PC Goldsmith, for they were both found on the same ley line and on land that had been thoroughly searched previously. In each case there were discrepancies in newspaper reportage, some giving the date of the Reverend's disappearance as 31 August 1978, others the 31 December 1978, whereas the correct date was 31 October 1978 – All Hallows Eve.

Father Snelling had been rector of Clapham and Patching for thirteen years from 1960 to 1974, retiring then to live in Steyning, and although he was known to suffer bouts of depression, he was said to be in good form on the day he disappeared, chatting to people in the 'bus to Goring where his dentist practised and generally projecting a cheery manner.

At the inquest held in August 1981, Mrs Vera Snelling, his widow, was able to identify the wallet and credit card together with a signet ring and watch found by the body, and pathologist Dr John Shore said that there was no sign of injury to the bones and that the skeleton had been almost complete. He had, however, noticed some metal gauze which suggested a hernia operation had been performed at some time and that teeth in the lower jaw had been recently extracted. The inquest heard that Father Snelling had indeed had as many as three hernia operations and also teeth recently extracted and the coroner, Mr Mark Calvert-Lee, said he was satisfied the remains were those of Mr Snelling.

He went on to say that it was possible he took a short cut through the woods to get home before dark, and that it was possible he tripped and injured himself or had a heart attack. 'But I have absolutely no evidence to help me,' he added, recording an open verdict.

But if he had suffered a fall and been unable to walk – although the inquest was told no bones had been broken – why was he not found before? Similarly, if he had suffered a heart attack, or even taken his own life – for which the coroner said there was no evidence whatsoever – why was his body not found sooner? That whole area had been thoroughly searched at the time of his disappearance and subsequently. If he had died from natural causes, *why* was he not found? Unless, of course, he happened not to have died where his remains were ultimately discovered. Could this be a possibility?

Imagine a deserted downland path with wisps of late afternoon mist rising in the still autumn air as dusk descends, bringing an aura of mystery to this pagan Sabbat of Hallowe'en. Into view comes an elderly man walking alone, hurrying a little, perhaps, in order to get home while there is still light enough to see. Add to this the fact that the man is an ordained priest of the Christian Church, still well-known despite his retirement, and easily recognisable walking the familiar paths near the bounds of his old parish. Then on that lonely path and coming from the opposite direction, someone else appears, someone who knows him and who is anti everything he stands for. What might happen next?

Several years before being appointed vicar of Clapham and Patching, Father Snelling, while overworking at a parish near Brighton had attempted to commit suicide, and having been chaplain to a rehabilitation unit for mental cases, he was

he sealed north door at Clapham church, a ure sign that villagers feared witchcraft and cult practices.

Strange tunnel of trees to the north of Clapham church whose dark proliferation of foliage seems to intensify the feeling of isolation experienced in this particular area.

Mysterious pit north of Clapham.

The demonic mural photographed by Charles Walker.

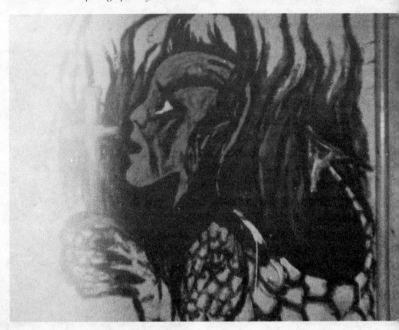

Charles Walker at the crossroads site in Clapham wood where he met an initiate of the Friends of Hecate one night in the autumn of 1978.

The site in Clapham wood where the Friends of Hecate are known to have met and held rituals.

The tree at the 'Crossroads' in Clapham wood close to the area where dogs disappeared and people have reported being overcome by unseen forces.

The north-east front of bizarre Castle Goring, the house with two faces, (the south-west front is in the Italian Palladin style), built for Shelley by his eccentric grandfather.

Mysterious tree stumps at Chanctonbury Ring, which disappeared as strangely as they had appeared and which were thought to be placed there for a Satanic ritual.

Black altar at Chanctonbury Ring, discovered by Charles Walker in 1979 and photographed by him.

well aware of the emotional crises and general hopelessness of some people's lives, prompting them to make such attempts.

Anxious to help such people in his work as a country parson, Father Snelling started an extension of the Samaritan telephone service in the Clapham area, advertising his 'phone number and bidding would-be suicides to contact him before they did anything rash. There is no doubt this new service filled a local need even from outside the sprawling parish, and met with a measure of success: there is no doubt, also, that it would not have been very well received by an anti-Christian group, especially worshippers of Hecate, bearing in mind she was Goddess of Untimely Deaths and Suicides. Whilst there is no evidence that it was suggested he discontinue this particular service, several parishioners noticed a certain tension mounting within the parish about this time, and Mr Bennett, a church-warden at Clapham, commented that Father Snelling was often seen walking about the village looking disturbed as if he had something else, much bigger, on his mind.

Did he suspect the existence of a secret Satanic cult practising within the bounds of his parish? And on the fateful day he disappeared, was he approached 'in the lurking places of the village' by someone who seized upon the chance for personal or sectarian revenge? Was he appealed to for help, enticed elsewhere on some pretext and, being a man of the cloth, went willingly if unsuspectingly with his killer? Afterwards the body could so easily have been hidden until all the hullabaloo died down, and then dumped on land previously searched in the restricted zone, to be found years after there was any possibility of ascertaining the true cause of death. What really happened?

Mrs Jillian Matthews

The following month, on 28 September 1981, Mrs Jillian Matthews, a 37-year-old divorcee, went missing from her home in Worthing. Under an arrangement for homeless people organised by the Social Services, she was being looked after by a friend, Mrs Marion Wolfe, who said that at 3 o'clock in the afternoon of the day she disappeared, Jillian Matthews went out for a walk to the shops saying she would return in about an hour. When she did not come back a search was instigated, with

Mrs Wolfe driving to Steyning, where Mrs Matthews's ex-husband lived, but no-one could throw any light on the reason for her disappearance.

It was not until six weeks later at noon on Saturday, 14 November, that her body was found on private land at Wiston by Mr Alan Budd from Clapham and Andrew Martin whilst beating for a pheasant shoot, who literally stumbled across it as it lay on the ground uncovered. The body, which was minus tights and pants, was lying about 60 yards from Spithandle Lane off the Ashington Road some five miles from Steyning, and Mr Anthony Flowers, head keeper of the North Wiston shoot whose hunt leases the land from nearby Wiston Estate, said 'Strangely enough we had been over the exact spot a fortnight before but had not seen anything.'

Detective Chief Superintendent Geoff Curd said that the police were treating it as a murder inquiry. 'It is going to be a tough case to crack because she has been dead for so long,' he remarked. Mrs Matthews's body was badly decomposed but tests revealed that she had been raped and strangled. Police spent the several days immediately after discovery of the body combing the area for clues including the missing articles of clothing, but found nothing, and in a statement issued on 25 November 1981 a police spokesman said, 'It is thought that there are a number of people in the Steyning area who are reluctant to speak directly to the police.' A confidential 'phone line was then set up with 40 more officers carrying out house to house enquiries, but as with PC Goldsmith and Father Snelling, all such enquiries proved fruitless.

Although Mrs Matthews was a woman with a rather low IQ who had been receiving treatment for schizophrenia, it was said that she had emerged from this completely cured and 'a different person'. According to Superintendent Curd she had become a social person, fastidious about her clothes, and had in fact just bought a new pair of black lace-up shoes which she was very excited about. They were found beside her body together with her handbag, but it was thought she had no money with her on the day she went missing.

It was revealed that she liked wandering about the countryside on her own and had in fact gone missing on other occasions, but always made a point of keeping in touch by telephone. It seemed unlikely that on the day of her disappearance she would have deliberately gone walking in woodland for fear of spoiling the new shoes of which she was so proud.

Despite extensive police enquiries her murderer remains at large, but there are so many similarities between her murder and the deaths of PC Goldsmith and Father Snelling that it would seem they must be connected, however tenuously. All three were believed to have been walking alone on the Downs in the Chanctonbury/Wiston/Steyning area which, like Clapham, is enmeshed with ley lines (running towards Devil's Dyke and Brighton in the east and connecting Cissbury and Clapham in the south and west); all three were found on private land which had been thoroughly searched previously but revealed nothing; all three were believed to be suffering from some degree of depression, although Mrs Matthews and Father Snelling were said to have been in good spirits on the days of their respective disappearances, and in each case – including that of Mr Foster who was recognisable only from his belongings although it was known he had been missing for less than a month – such extensive and unusual body decomposition had taken place that the causes of death were impossible to ascertain.

WISTON HOUSE – SEAT OF EUROPEAN CONFERENCES

Wiston House is a stately Elizabethan mansion tucked away in the seclusion of its own extensive woodland of some 7,000 acres situate on the South Downs near Steyning. Half of its acreage is now devoted to farms with over 150 homes on the estate, the rest comprising two chalkpits, two sandpits and woodland.

Its history goes back to Saxon times, and at the time of Domesday, Wistanestun, as it was known in 1086, was owned by William de Braose. Then a medieval manor set in woodland, it passed through marriage into the Shelley family when a descendant of William's, namely John de Braose, died without a male heir. Sir Robert Shelley promptly had it torn down and replaced in 1576 by the splendid Elizabethan mansion it is today. However, when the family got heavily into debt through their support of Charles the First, the Shelleys were forced to sell out, unhappily to a member of the very tribunal that had tried the king, one Sir John Fagge.

In 1743, again through marriage, Wiston House passed to Sir John Goring whose family owned it for some two hundred years, and it was Charles Goring who planted the beech trees on Chanctonbury Ring.

Since 1949, Wiston has been the home of the Wilton Park Conferences and, more recently, of the European Discussion Centre. The Wilton Park Conferences were first started after World War 2 by the late Sir Heinz Köeppler who had the idea of closing the gap between war-torn nations and bringing together, in England, young Germans who had grown up under Hitler ignorant of democracy, to listen to prominent people talking on relevant subjects, and it was a resounding success. Although in about 1957 the Government tried to close it down, there was so much reaction, especially from the Germans, that they decided to extend it to other countries, and in a short space of time it drew participants from 25 different countries and now includes the European Discussion Centre. 'There is no doubt that the Wilton Park Conferences contributed greatly to, and had a high influence on the present German democratic system,' said Mr Alan Hughes, deputy director of the Wiston House Centre in April 1980.

The discussions, which are said to be informal, cover a wide range of subjects including political matters, although it is denied that there is any specific political bias, and those taking part are – to quote a spokesman – 'People who have been to the conferences before and who are about five years short of the top, that is those who may now have become prime ministers and top businessmen in their own countries and who consequently count as regards British prestige abroad.' All conferences are said to be 'strictly off the record', and the main conference room is fitted out for simultaneous interpretation with microphones, headphones and interpreters. Up to 1980 these discussions were only open to Common Market countries, but it was envisaged that this would be altered to include a far more international programme.

Much secrecy appears to surround Wiston House, especially the way it recruits people for its conferences, although the German Foreign Office have taken it upon themselves to find suitable participants in its sphere, but after a conference held on security and defence at which over 40 per cent of the participants were military personnel, nearby Steyning was rife with rumour and speculation as to what exactly was going on in this stately old mansion set in their midst.

If, as has been announced, its object is to be 'the heart and soul of a unique international network that aims at strengthening world relations by nurturing greater co-operation and understanding', then surely nothing should be allowed to interfere with this noble concept. Is it mere coincidence that a secret Satanic group whose aims and influences are the exact opposite, should be practising in such close proximity?

8 THE FACELESS ONES

'Words ought to be a little wild for they are the assault of thoughts on the unthinking.'

J.M. Keynes

'But I am forbid
To tell the secrets of my prison-house,
I could a tale unfold whose lightest word
Would harrow up thy soul, freeze thy young blood,'

Shakespeare
Hamlet, I

BEHIND THE MASK OF ANONYMITY

Publication of my three articles on the mysteries of Clapham Wood and Chanctonbury Ring in the magazine *The Unexplained* engendered quite a lot of interest and brought me considerable correspondence. These letters were forwarded to me by the publishers, usually in batches at a time: those addressed to the magazine having been dealt with by the editorial staff and sent on to me for information, whereas those addressed personally to me were forwarded unopened. Amongst one of these batches was an anonymous letter, ill-typed, unsigned and couched in words 'a little wild', but which nevertheless bore the unmistakable stamp of authenticity.

Not only did this letter provide some answers to the questions I had posed in my articles, but it also confirmed the existence of the group calling themselves the Friends of Hecate – the writer spelt it 'Hekate' – who were 'much more than a black coven'. So far as my researchers and I were concerned, this information in the opening paragraph alone authenticated the letter-writer for us, for there was no way he or she could have known the name of the group except through first-hand knowledge. A Satanic group does not allow its name to be bandied about willy-nilly, and I had specifically not mentioned their name in any of my published articles as our sole source of information had been the initiate who volunteered the name of the group during his clandestine meeting with Charles Walker. The letter-writer, therefore, can only have come upon this information in a similar way, that is by personal contact.

As will be seen from the reproduction of the anonymous letter, the writer claims that a friend of his (hers?) had joined the Friends of Hecate and that they met in Clapham Woods and the barn by the church and made ritual sacrifices at the time of Orion and The Archer.

The barn mentioned is the one in which Charles took the photograph of the demonic mural which was painted on its west wall, and the ritual sacrifices confirm the initiate's claim that dogs and farm animals were used for this purpose.

With regard to the meetings occurring at the time of Orion and The Archer, the Orion constellation is prominent in the winter sky peaking in December, and the sun passes through Sagittarius (The Archer) from mid-December to mid-January, reaching its farthest point south at the time of the Winter Solstice, 21–22 December. From this it would seem that the preference is to hold meetings during the autumn and winter, which also coincides with the shooting season.

The writer goes on to say:

'Lots of Patching and Clapham people are in it but the top ones come from London, two women and a man, the man is a doctor, about 45, the women about 30 and 60. They always go back to London after the meetings so no one knows who they are or that they are connected with what goes on,'

and then comes the chilling rider:

'I think this is when there is a human sacrifice.'

The writer may not have been in the complete confidence of his or her friend, but knew enough to draw some pertinent conclusions. The implications are ugly indeed.

Details are given next as regards other similar groups in Winchester and Avebury and a 'big group in London', and that:

'lots of people are involved as there are different grades, and thousands of members in the outer one but only about 200 at the inner circle. It is all very secret, the inner core members are protected by the others who they use as spies and guards to make sure everything is kept secret.'

The latter comments are borne out by Charles Walker's recent experience when he was stopped twice in different places by men bearing shotguns whilst he was out walking one evening in Clapham Wood. A security force in the form of armed wardens or gamekeepers to ensure absolute privacy could be quite legitimately organised where the exclusive shooting rights had been leased or purchased. Is this how a secret cult such as the Friends of Hecate has been able to operate so successfully all these years and able to carry on its nefarious practices relatively untroubled by any interference from either land-owners or outsiders? Although a party of people gathering together in woodland during the shooting season occasions no comment, what has been remarked upon by local people is the shooting party's apparent lack of prowess in this particular field of sport. My contact in Clapham told me:

'People who have purchased exclusive shooting rights from the privately owned estates come down from London. Big money changes hands and they don't bag many birds. I know, because I've seen them.'

Are exclusive shooting rights held merely as a cover, therefore?

It will be recalled that Mrs Jillian Matthews's body was found by beaters for a shoot on land that had been leased from the Wiston Estate for exclusive shooting rights. PC Goldsmith's body was found – also by beaters – in the same area. Father Snelling's remains were discovered in a Ministry of Defence restricted zone within which is Wiston House, used for European Conferences and categorised Top Secret, and even the body of Mr Leon Foster was found at Clapham in woodland leased out for shooting.

If the organisation is as large as the anonymous letter writer suggests, the skilful legal manipulation of land-owners in this way could mean that the land-owners, estate workers, government employees, beaters, etc., would remain in complete ignorance of what was really going on in private lands throughout the country. In this way, secrecy could be maintained practically indefinitely.

The writer refers to the Patching and Clapham membership numbering about 30, in which case the group calling itself the Friends of Hecate probably exists as a single cell. In company with other similar cells throughout the country, each possibly having a different name, it appears to be controlled by an inner circle centred in London (or Winchester) with a triad of adepts holding overall power at its nucleus.

The younger woman mentioned, aged about 30 years, would probably be the high priestess, for although, as the letter writer says, the Friends of Hecate are 'much more than a black coven', the general *modus operandi* would more than likely be based on ritualistic Satanism combined, probably, with certain other innovations embracing occult practices more specifically slanted to the demands of the Hecate cult. Perhaps the innovator of this was the older woman mentioned, now aged about 60 years. At the time it is believed the group was formed in Sussex – during the 1960s – there was immense interest by people from all walks of life in matters appertaining to mysticism and the occult, including an Aleister Crowley revival, renewed interest in witchcraft both black and white, and psychic phenomena.

Nowadays, the older woman would probably be acting in an advisory position as her occult knowledge would be invaluable to the group, and as regards the third member of the triad – a doctor – it seems a skilled medic is a most valuable acquisition insofar as both black and white covens are concerned. With a group such as the Friends of Hecate, whose cult – according to the initiate – demands a blood sacrifice to be made at each meeting they hold, medical expertise would be essential, especially if the more sinister aspects of ritual sacrifice were involved as the anonymous letter-writer so gruesomely implies.

'He was sick of it all', the writer continues about the friend's complicity, adding that he was 'very frightened' when the police were searching for the vicar, and the inference here is that the friend either knew, or suspected, that something untoward had befallen the missing man for whom everyone at that time was so diligently searching.

With regard to the variety of strange feelings which people

visiting Clapham Woods have said they experienced, the letter-writer attributes these to a 'force wall' that 'can be left about'. This appears to be a power emanating from a black magic ritual, such as a remnant from one of their rites, or a deliberately invoked elemental, which would have the effect of keeping people away and ensuring the continued privacy of the cult. There is no doubt that such an irresponsible practice could be harmful for anyone stumbling unknowingly into such a presence. Recalling the words of Elymas, high priest of a Brighton coven: 'When we perform a ritual we make sure that when we have finished we remove any elemental we may have raised,' and this seems to be the caring code of practice generally applied to *Wicca*. However, taking into consideration the letter-writer's comment that 'the place is right for building up the best vibrations', it could be that the Friends of Hecate use Clapham as a proving ground for neophytes and initiates before they are admitted to the higher echelons of the group.

In this connection, it will be remembered that during the clandestine meeting in 1978, the initiate told Charles Walker, 'We have been using this area for ten years and plan to continue using it for another ten, after which time we will select other areas in which to spread the word'. Is this what is happening now? Are they expanding nationwide? As all the Clapham phenomena, UFO activities, disappearing dogs, etc., peaked in the 1970s, has this specific area in the Rape of Bramber served its immediate purpose?

As regards expansion, the country is full of land-owners feeling the economic pinch and therefore only too willing to lease their lands or grant exclusive shooting rights, especially if, as my Clapham informant says, 'Big money changes hands'. So a highly organised group having the necessary clout – financial and otherwise – on all social levels including, no doubt, the aristocracy, would experience little difficulty in implementing a programme of rapid growth and extending their dubious activities into selected rural areas commensurate with the ideal conditions existing at Clapham.

The anonymous letter-writer says of the group: 'They can make people do what they want', and that they can 'break people's resistance mentally so as to get control of them and situations.'

If this is so, it would involve a power akin to that developed and practised by malefic magicians, well-known in worldwide sorcery. The collective focusing of a destructive force has long been a facet of diabolical witchcraft and black magic (not to be confused with the beneficent neopagan witchcraft practised by present-day white witches) for which African witch doctors were renowned, though by no means exclusively. All countries, from the Australian Aborigine 'pointing the bone' to the Haitian necromantic branch of Voodoo known as *Culte des Mortes*, can boast of some kind of hostile magic.

The manipulation, and specific directing, of this dark side of occult power, if used on any large scale such as is inferred by the letter-writer, would undoubtedly have far-reaching social and political effects, and such a concept could only be embraced by a well-organised group led by highly skilled adepts well-versed in all aspects of occult practices. It seems that the anonymous letter-writer's concluding remarks: 'They are much more powerful than a black coven' is a very perceptive observation.

So what sort of group are the Friends of Hecate and are there any historical parallels?

THE HELLFIRE CLUB

During the eighteenth century a demonic brotherhood composed of distinguished intellectuals came into being: politicians and wealthy eccentrics drawn from the highest reaches of English society. They dressed up as monks and met at Medmenham Abbey in Buckinghamshire, presided over by Sir Francis Dashwood who had leased the ancient abbey and turned it into his personal 'palace of delights'. Its members met only at night, and in secret – sometimes in the natural underground caves of High Wycombe – but mostly conducting their devil-worship and holding their debaucheries of 'food, drink, gaming and sex' in the elegant surroundings of Medmenham Abbey.

As their basic activities were partially rooted in the heretic practices of the London Hellfire clubs of an earlier period – though the Medmenham Monks were far more dedicated to Luciferian worship than these earlier blasphemers who frequented London's old taverns and they should not be confused with them – they were more commonly known as 'The Hellfire Club', and the most notorious Satanists of their day.

(The Old English word, *Hel*, meaning 'underworld', is also

the name of the Norse Goddess of Death, and the Germanic *haljo*, meaning 'hidden place'. In addition to these are the Latin *celare* 'to conceal' and *occulere*, 'to hide', from which we get our word 'occult' meaning 'hidden'.)

The membership list of The Hellfire Club makes quite impressive reading, and amongst the more important members were Dashwood's friend, Lord Sandwich; the wealthy son of the Archbishop of Canterbury, Thomas Potter, whose participation in the orgies reduced him to a gouty and palsied wreck; Potter's friend, George Selwyn, who apparently indulged in the quaint habit of attending executions disguised as an old woman; Paul Whitehead, a spendthrift married to a rich half-wit; the Marquis of Bute; another odd character by the name of George Bubb Dodington who had inherited a fortune and whose large Jacobean house in London's fashionable Hammersmith was named 'La Trappe' after the Cistercian abbey at Soligny la Trappe in France; John Wilkes, a well-known politician and champion of the underdog, and his friend, Charles Churchill.

Self-styled monks, many of them were connected with the Opposition party in the House of Commons, and these public figures of the mid-1700s delighted in donning monastic habits and gathering together in Sir Francis Dashwood's Satanically decorated ruined abbey, together with many of the local gentry, to conduct their Satanic rites and indulge in the special festivities of the brotherhood.

Part of their organisation consisted of a 'Superior Order of 12' and an 'Inferior Order of 12', the latter being composed of less important members whilst the Superior Order included the prime movers in the brotherhood who each adopted secret names (Dashwood being known as *St* Francis) and whose activities were kept highly secret. In fact it was only the members of this Superior Order who were permitted to enter the chapel of Medmenham where they held their Satanic rites amidst a suitably profane setting bedecked with pornographic pictures. Sometimes, however, a new member of the brotherhood would be baptised to Lucifer in these imaginative surroundings, when an inversion of the orthodox liturgy would be used, and by all accounts the ceremonies and Satanic practices were taken seriously, especially by the elite membership of the 'Superior Order of 12'.

By 1762, the majority of the Superior Order of the Hellfire

Club were in political power. Bute was Prime Minister, Dashwood was Chancellor of the Exchequer, and even Bubb Dodington rose to Cabinet rank, whilst John Wilkes and his friend Charles Churchill found themselves on the Opposition benches. Perhaps it was this political abyss as much as anything that prompted Wilkes to plot to expose the secret Satanic society of which he had obviously become a very disgruntled member.

He engineered this most humorously by concealing an ape equipped with artificial horns and dressed in a long black cloak in a box, and releasing it during one of 'St Francis's' Satanic ceremonies. The sudden appearance of this devil bounding about in their midst can best be imagined, but in the melee that followed, Lord Sandwich apparently fell to the floor screaming for mercy when the 'devil' fastened itself upon him, and it was some time before he could be rescued from the attentions of the amorous ape.

After this debacle Medmenham Abbey could no longer be used, and the brotherhood later dispersed. Although for a time Dashwood tried to continue the society, the secrecy surrounding it had been too thoroughly exploded, and Medmenham Abbey became merely an object of curiosity and he an object of ridicule. He contented himself instead by building on Wycombe Hill a secular church surmounted by a golden ball and equipped within with wine bins. Here he would imbibe his favourite milk punch whilst roaring out parodies of the Psalms. He died in 1781 – but did the inherent nature of the infamous Hellfire Club die with him or was it left in trust for those practitioners of Satanism who would be bound to follow?

PRACTITIONERS OF SATANISM

Those sufficiently interested in demonic and Satanic practices to join a relevant group usually manage to keep that interest so well concealed that even members of their own family are unaware of their activities. They live their everyday lives like most other people and there is nothing in their physiognomy or in their outward behaviour to betray where their baser sentiments truly lie.

According to our research, devil worship has been practised in Clapham and the Rape of Bramber for a thousand years, albeit intermittently, by a diversity of people from the humble peasants who, as Jeffrey B. Russell says, 'practised sorcery in order to improve their own position at the expense of their neighbours, or simply to exercise their spite', to the highly organised groups of wealthy intellectuals making sacrifices to their chosen deity and invoking Satan.

By whatever term such practices are known, whether devil worship, Satanism, diabolic witchcraft or Black Magic, and no matter which particular demon or deity is worshipped, they all have one end result in common: the specific benefit of the worshippers. And this is nearly always inimical to others.

Was it any accident that members of the Hellfire Club held top Government positions? Unless one is gullible enough to believe it was mere coincidence, some dire influence must have been brought to bear somewhere along the line to ensure their attainment of such political power. When one reflects that the three who attained highest office were all members of the most secret inner circle or 'Superior Order' as it was known, it seems evident that some pretty hefty demonic strings were pulled to facilitate their lust for power.

Today the Friends of Hecate also seem intent on political persuasion, for not only does the anonymous letter-writer point this out but Julio Caro Baroja's statement that 'Hecate is a deity around whom secret cults and ideas of terror could easily develop' also confirms the parallels which exist between the modern cult and the notorious Hellfire Club of old.

These political overtones could put them in quite a different league to other groups who seem content to combine devotion to sensual pleasures with a theatrical kind of occultism, whereas the type of worship apparently being practised by the Friends of Hecate does not seem to have been previously chronicled, but by all accounts is a particularly virulent form.

In other ways, too, they seem unlike the general run of occult groups, for whilst most cults associated with diabolic witchcraft work with the moon, the Hecate-inspired group use the stars and planetary positions as well as tapping in to the ley system and the corruptive influence of the 'black streams'. Their apparent mastery of this combination of cosmic power with the natural earth forces not only implies adherence to a very old condition of worship probably having its roots in druidism, but by their experimentation and expertise in the hidden realms of thought, the power they could wield for ill would be immense.

In his book *Supernature* written in 1971, Dr Lyall Watson says:

'Our future lies in the mind and in our understanding of it, but the intricate rituals and ceremonies that once surrounded occult practices associated with the powers of the mind may surprise us and turn out to have direct effects of their own. Matter, mind, and magic are all one in the cosmos.'

And it is this future – *our* future – which these practitioners of Satanism appear to be so categorically pledged to influence for their own ends.

MALEFIC POWER SPIRAL

This is the method of organisation which has been employed by the more powerful occult orders for centuries because it serves a dual purpose: that of adequately training neophytes in the secret pursuits of the cult and that of ensuring continued secrecy and total security in respect of the cult as a whole and all its members.

Absolute secrecy is an inherent part of any clandestine sect or subversive faction; there are no half measures. Complete anonymity of the individual is one of the prerequisites of membership, for only by subordinating himself utterly and unquestioningly to the dictates of the controlling hierarchy does the neophyte obtain initial acceptance, and in so doing forfeits any personal considerations. Whatever opinions he may have held he is now 'one of them', and whatever he is required to do he does in the name of the cult. So however badly things may turn out for him, however disillusioned he may become with his 'prison-house' as he ascends the spiral of power and gets more and more involved in the innermost activities of the cult, there can be no retraction, no escape; membership of any such group is a one-way ticket.

The late Dion Fortune, an authority on Occultism, advised caution before one joined any such group, saying

'One occult organisation is well known to have been involved in the drug traffic, another is riddled with unnatural vice ... others have been involved in subversive politics. Those who join fraternities without properly investigating them and the credentials of those who are running them may find themselves involved in any or all of these things. Behind the veil of secrecy, guarded by impressive oaths, many things may happen, and it is therefore essential to inform oneself most carefully concerning the character, credentials and record of the leaders of the organisation.'

Information such as this, however, is rarely forthcoming, and it is often only through bitter experience that the member eventually realises what he has got himself into.

Integral with the worship of a deity is the concept of blood sacrifice, which has been practised throughout the world for centuries, and still is today. It is not necessarily confined to those groups with Satanic propensities; during their ritual ceremonies the druid priesthood practised it, and theirs is believed to have been a religion essentially of nature worship. Blood is the prime factor in human sacrifice, underlying which – according to Dion Fortune – are two entirely different ideas. One is the willing sacrifice, the other the unwilling.

The first entails the concept of divine union with the chosen god, the willing victim being either a priest or devotee seeking such mystical alliance. The other type of human sacrifice involves a captive, probably drugged into passivity, whose sacrifice is not, as is generally thought, made to propitiate the gods but in order that his vital life forces may serve as a basis of manifestation. Thus the life energies would be transmuted to make up the manifested entity. This type of ceremonial high black magic would only be witnessed, or indeed only known about, by adepts at the very core of the cult, and it is doubtful whether anyone below the 'top power spiral' would ever become aware of such practices.

Whilst it is not known how the Friends of Hecate enrol and promote initiates and organise their internal affairs, it could be based on the Spiral of Power method of occult organisation comprised of seven rings or coils. Neophytes fully vetted and accepted as suitable would start on the outer ring. They would probably attend meetings policed by initiates from higher up, who would note their progress and potential usefulness. The rituals at these outer fringe meetings would be designed to tantalise and give the would-be initiates a taste of more to come without ever divulging exactly what. Thus the potential initiates would be witnessing the vulgarities as opposed to the obscenities,

112

which is quite different, and as they became more useful to the group and ascended the spiral, so would they become more and more tainted. When it was seen that they could be fully trusted and had developed the mental prowess and disciplines necessary to participate in the group's activities, they might then be taken into the confidence of the inner circle, but this would be the closest they would ever be likely to get to the office of high priest, at the very heart of the cult.

At this level, the new inner circle members would become totally committed, which means that from being mere thrill-seekers wishing to dabble, they could find themselves sucked into a Satanic whirlpool which holds them inextricably for life, rendering them for all time ... The Faceless Ones.

*   *   *   *   *

Note. My researchers and I have discussed at great length the *bona fides* of the anonymous letter-writer, and whilst, as I have stated in this chapter, his or her knowledge regarding the name of the cult alone authenticated, for us, the contents of the letter, the identity of the writer remains a puzzle. It seems highly unlikely, to us, that an initiate or trusted member of the cult would be able to disappear abroad, as the anonymous letter-writer suggests, unless he or she had made some watertight plans in secret and carried them out with speed and precision. Is it possible, therefore, that the letter-writer and his or her friend *and* the initiate who spoke to Charles Walker, are one and the same person?

Or, again, is there someone in the full confidence of the inner circle who despite their involvement has managed to retain his or her mental equilibrium, but, sickened by what is happening, felt impelled to break silence? As with party politics, the politics of fear can beget such powerful emotions that relief can often only be obtained by leaking what is secretly known.

So although we may never know the identify of the letter-writer – and indeed have no wish to know – the fact that they communicated anonymously should not detract from the letter's content, prompted as it undoubtedly was by the revulsion for Satanic practices which the writer felt.

*   *   *   *   *

9 LINKS WITH THE SUB-ETHER

'The awful shadow of some unseen Power
Floats through unseen among us, – visiting
This various world with as inconstant wing
As summer winds that creep from flower to flower.'

Percy Bysshe Shelley
'Hymn to Intellectual Beauty'

'The angels keep their ancient places; –
Turn but a stone, and start a wing!
'Tis ye, 'tis your estrangèd faces,
That miss the many-splendoured thing.'

Francis Thompson
'The Kingdom of God'

THE ORPHIC COSMOGONY
That there are worlds parallel to ours containing life forms
evolving at different vibratory levels and time frequencies and
which impinge upon the earth, has been the profound belief of
psychics and seers from ancient times. Scientifically unproven,
it remains but an unlikely concept to the analytical scientific
mind as well as to the 'doubting Thomas', both of whom are so
often openly cynical and always requiring proof.

The cosmogony attributed to Orpheus, the Thracian musician
and poet, held that the first principle of the universe was Cronos
(or Time) from which came Chaos, symbolising infinite space,
and Ether, the creative principle.

Ether is hypothetical because unseen. It is everywhere, and is
the invisible substance permeating earth by which heat, light
and electro-magnetic waves are transmitted and is, by the same

token, the fluidic substance of the spheres of spirit through which emanations appear.

According to Orpheus, Chaos was surrounded by Night, which formed the enveloping cover under which, by the creative action of Ether, cosmic matter was slowly organised. Night became the shell of the immense egg which was formulated after eons of time, and whose upper section was the vault of the sky, and whose lower was Earth (*Ge*, land, or *Gaia*, goddess of earth).

When the three sons of Cronos drew lots for the partitioning of the Earth, Zeus received as his share the sublime regions of the Ether, for which rulership the Cyclopes gave him the thunderbolt; Poseidon was given rulership of the tumultuous sea, for which he was given a trident; whilst the third son, Hades, received a helmet of darkness or invisibility to mark his rulership of the sombre depths of the Earth.

It is these 'sombre depths' that have fascinated mankind since the beginning of time, this 'otherworld' being populated with all manner of strange entities, and whilst it is not possible in a brief chapter to do more than touch upon this vast subject, it is an indisputable fact that most people, when pressed, readily agree that it exists, and that there is something – indefinable, perhaps – beyond the generally accepted physical bounds which can be either Shelley's 'awful shadow of some unseen Power', or Thompson's 'many-splendoured thing', according to its level of emanation.

Among the many contemporary schools of thought concerning parallel worlds, the most popular concept is the promulgation that there are three simultaneous planetary realities of existence:

(i) The Lower Planes of the physical earth.
(ii) The Middle Planes of the sub-ether or 'otherworld' which harbours demi-gods (part-spiritual and part-physical beings), and which is itself sub-divided into two zones, one reached by the good Right-hand Path (Light) and the other via the evil, Left-hand Path (Darkness).
(iii) The Upper Planes which are ethereal and pure spirit.

It is believed by some that the Holy Trinity is reflected in these three levels, the Father as the Godhead being on the Upper

Planes, the Holy Ghost representative of the Middle Planes, and the Christ made incarnate as mortal man on the Lower Planes. Be that as it may, it is more generally accepted that all three levels support different life forms, and that it is the occult Middle Planes which, in the first instance, the Adepts contact during ritualistic high magic ceremonies.

THE DEVA KINGDOM

'The Middle Plane of Horrors' is how the Hindus describe the sub-ethereal world because it is neither one thing nor the other. It is belonging and yet not belonging. It is existing and yet not existing. They believe it to be a battleground of part-physical and part-spiritual demi-gods serving either the Lords of Light or the Lords of Darkness in a twilight zone inhabited by unimaginable beings. It is also thought to be a staging-post for souls in transit.

Deva was a Hindu god – a good spirit – and his sub-ethereal kingdom is shared, amongst others, with the Elementals or Nature Spirits, each group of which represents one of the four earthly elements of Fire, Water, Air and Earth. As Elementals, these Nature Spirits are required to do the bidding of others, whose intentions can be either good or evil. Thus Fire can warm or burn, Water can quench or drown, Air can be pure or foul, and Earth can support or smother.

Some human beings, especially those of a refined and sensitive nature, have a great fascination for the Elementals, finding in them a stimulating source of inspiration and with whom they feel an undoubted empathy. The emotionally immature and mentally unstable also seem to be instinctively drawn towards the elemental kingdom, contact with whom can exacerbate their condition and lead to obsession. Not because the Elementals are bad in themselves, but they are 'profoundly disturbing to the human consciousness' according to Dion Fortune, who advises that only an initiate using the established rituals should attempt to get in touch with them or any other inhabitants of this twilight world.

Dion Fortune further postulates the fascinating idea that these non-human elementals can be drawn into our world at the moment of conception should the female be severely under the influence of heavy drugs or alcohol at the time. Whilst this seems to be the exception rather than the rule, it would explain why, on rare occasions, we come up against a person who is charming in a cold, china doll-like way but seems entirely lacking in the normal human emotions, for the resultant child of the drug-influenced union can grow into a charming and fascinating person but appears devoid of the milk of human kindness and can seem almost soulless in its actions and attitudes towards other human beings. This could be because, although having taken human form, the person is basically a one-element creature (human beings comprise all four elements) and has no equipment or experience to assimilate or control the other three elements. Dion Fortune adds, 'We must not allow the human form to mislead us as to the existence of a human soul.'

However, whilst preoccupation with certain aspects of the Deva Kingdom may serve to delay and distort the human evolution, the sub-ether's natural influence over the earth on which it impinges, is considerable. 'Any organic geographical unit develops something of an oversoul and where the differentiation is marked, the oversoul may become a very definite entity,' Dion Fortune maintains. This idea is reflected in Professor Lovelock's 'Gaian' hypothesis where the planet is seen as a single self-monitoring organism, a concept embraced by many of today's ecologically biased thinkers. Paul Devereux extends this further by wondering if the planet can also dream – such dreaming obviously producing images that would most likely be zoomorphic and anthropomorphic in expression. 'Perhaps,' he says, 'this is where the images of 'elementals' and 'devas' come from.' Perhaps, too, the strange yet naturally occurring force which flows along the ley lines that criss-cross the Earth emanates from this sub-ethereal sphere as does its related power of electro-magnetism.

If Man persists in tampering with these unknown forces he should certainly never lose sight of their seemingly volatile origin, and it behoves him to tread very carefully in the realms of experimentation. If he does not, he could unleash forces he knows not how to cope with, as happened in an American experiment that went badly wrong in 1943.

THE BIZARRE TRAGEDY OF THE *ELDRIDGE*
The story of this United States naval destroyer has been well documented in a book by Charles Berlitz and William Moore

entitled *The Philadelphia Experiment*, and whilst I do not intend detailing its scientific nature, what little can be gleaned about this highly secret experiment is too pertinent to the subject matter of this book to be excluded.

In November 1943 the *USS Eldridge* was on convoy duties in the mid-Atlantic together with her sister ship the *USS Furuseth*. Aboard this latter vessel was a man calling himself Carl M. Allen who wrote several letters to a scientific journalist telling how he had witnessed a horrifying experiment aboard the *USS Eldridge*.

The scientific journalist, Morris K. Jessup, was at that time involved in writing about Einstein's theory of the unified field, and had made public his intention to fully investigate and report upon it, as it was to do with hitherto unknown forces which, it seemed, might explain – amongst other things – certain aspects of the UFO phenomena.

Implicit in Carl M. Allen's letters to Jessup was the repeated warning that he should have nothing to do with Einstein's theory but should immediately abandon the research for his own safety. In due course Jessup managed to trace the letter-writer to a New England county, and whilst he found that the man's real name was Carlos Allende, he also received confirmation that he had in fact served aboard the *Furuseth* and had sailed in company with the *Eldridge* at the time of the convoy. These facts, released by the US Authorities, signified to Jessup that the frightening details of the experiment the man said he witnessed could well be true.

In his first letter, Carlos Allende claimed to have seen the destroyer momentarily vanish, all except the ship's hull which had taken on a ghostly appearance, and in his second letter, Allende maintained that he had seen the experiment repeated when the *Eldridge* had returned to her home port in Philadelphia. On this occasion, however, there was a difference, for the ship had completely disappeared for a fraction of time and when she reappeared moments later most of her crew were found to be dead and those who had survived had become insane.

Allende named the man who would 'know all there is to know' about what happened aboard the *Eldridge* as Mr Franklin Reno, who, in 1939–40, had been working on a top-level project designed to utilise intense magnetic fields aboard ships in an attempt to deflect torpedoes and mines. The US Navy Department admitted that this type of research had in fact taken place, but maintained that it had been abandoned in 1941 due to the great cost involved. Whilst researching their book, the authors of *The Philadelphia Experiment* had interviewed Franklin Reno who had prematurely retired 'after the trouble' to the seclusion of America's mid-west.

He told them that the principles of 'hostile rejection' required a huge coil to be placed around the hull of a ship and fed an enormous negative charge which would create a magnetic field so powerful that no metallic intruder could resist its repellant force. Franklin Reno said he had repeatedly warned the Naval 'top-brass' that should the field be too intense, there was a risk of molecular disturbance occurring to the fabric of the ship, but despite his warnings, which he was told were 'noted', the experiment went ahead.

'They still watch me, you know,' Reno is reported to have told the authors, adding that, 'Maybe I know too much for my own good.'

It seems he was right, for a few months later he was found to have died in suspicious circumstances although he was officially reported as having died from natural causes.

A similar fate befell the journalist to whom Allende had written, Morris K. Jessup, who was found dead on 20 April 1959 in his station wagon, the engine still running and a length of pipe leading into his car from the exhaust. His close friends refused to believe the possibility of suicide. He was excited, they said, at the prospect of 'soon pulling the wool from the public's eyes', and it certainly seems most unlikely that, practically on the eve of his making such disclosures, he would suddenly take his own life. If he had indeed done so, it was a most fortuitous happening for those involved in the conspiracy of silence which obviously surrounded this experiment that went badly wrong.

After the second abortive experiment in the *Eldridge*'s home port, according to Allende's letters, the crew were found to be in a terrible state. 'Little sense could be gotten from them,' he wrote, and he told of men who 'shrieked and cried' when others approached them and of a sailor who had walked through a wall into nothingness and was never seen again. Many sailors had been set alight and burnt in a matter of seconds whilst those that survived had to be treated for third degree burns. Apparently, at enormous cost which the Navy Department justified as being 'normal servicing', an attempt was made to stabilise the ship and her company, but all to no avail, and the luckless *Eldridge* was eventually scrapped and her dire secrets lost for ever.

The US Authorities have always vehemently denied that the experiment ever took place; those who could throw light on it have died in suspicious circumstances, and as for Carlos Allende whose pseudonymous letters triggered off the investigation into the whole sorry business, no trace of him has ever been found.

So what really happened to the *Eldridge* and the men aboard her? Could this experiment-that-never-happened have been a clumsy attempt at dematerialisation? (It was ascertained that during the fractional moments she disappeared from her home port in Philadelphia she was reported to have materialised momentarily in her other dock at Newport News, Norfolk, which is some 300 miles distant.) Had Einstein's theory of the unified field become reality?

Apparently he spent the last 20 years of his life working on it, his argument being that the four major forces – gravity, electro-magnetism, strong nuclear and weak nuclear – could all be scientifically proven to be one and the same thing in a broad sense. He succeeded in linking the first two, and scientists at the Cern Institute in Switzerland linked weak nuclear with both magnetism and gravity, an experiment which reportedly cost some forty million pounds and produced atomic particles that have a life of one billionth of a second.

If intense magnetic fields can alter the atomic structure of matter, the atoms would be temporarily released from the effects of gravity, and on this premise the case of the *Eldridge* would be a distinct possibility. To the men aboard that ship at the time, the sudden burst of energy would be utterly devastating to their frail bodies, for not only would they suffer physically, especially from burns, but also their brain structure would be so completely displaced that they could be mentally deranged for life. At the moment of the power surge, released from the physical laws governing the Earth, it is theoretically possible they were 'flipped' into another dimension.

Is this what happened to the luckless crew? Were they all momentarily flung, in this abnormal fashion, into the world of the sub-ether, to experience in one split second of chaos the 'Horrors of the Middle Planes' and have the constitution of their minds destroyed in the process?

Perhaps no-one will ever admit that this is what really took place, but there is a sequel to this bizarre story, which Alan Brown heard about quite by chance from a friend of his.

THE PENITENT HITCH-HIKER

During the 1960s, Alan's friend was touring the West Country and happened to give a lift to an American hitch-hiker who wanted to go to Stonehenge. He appeared to be an utter physical wreck, sweating profusely, constantly fidgeting and jabbering nervously about his naval life aboard a ship named the *Eldridge*. He also said he had to wander the world visiting all the holy sites 'in penance', and by the time Alan's friend deposited him in the vicinity of Stonehenge, he realised the poor man was 'as mad as a hatter'.

The last he saw of the penitent hitch-hiker was the man running, arms outstretched, towards the ancient stone circle crying 'My God! My God!'

Was he one of the *Eldridge*'s survivors, belonging and yet not belonging, existing and yet not existing, a human being rendered an alien on Earth by the scientific experiment that went wrong? We shall never know, of course, because the experiment officially never happened.

10 IN PURSUIT OF POWER

'Unlimited power is apt to corrupt the minds of those who possess it.'

William Pitt
Speech in the House of Lords, 1770

THE SECRET POWER OF THE SUBTERRANEAN PEOPLES

'Non omnia possumus omnes'
'All power is not to all'

Virgil
Eclogues, viii

Lost Worlds

The force which power-thirsty Adepts are endeavouring to harness (for good or ill) is called *Prana* by the Hindus and has many other names, the most potent form of it being known to the Lamas of Tibet as *Vril*.

There are believed to be eight facets associated with the total control of *Pranic* or *'Vril*-power', the most important being named *Garima*, which is the ability to alter the shape of matter.

In his strange and fascinating book *The Coming Race*, the British author Edward Bulwer Lord Lytton credits the *Vril-ya*, an intellectual super-race of subterranean peoples, as having mastered *'Vril*-power', their ultimate aim being to rise up from their underground realms and take control of the world.

Lytton was born into a rich and privileged background in 1803 and as a young child was drawn to the world of the supernatural, evincing particular interest in the portrait of an ancestor of his, Dr John Bulwer, who in his day had studied mysticism and alchemy. Lytton was educated at Cambridge and inherited his title on his mother's death in 1838. He was by then deeply involved in occult studies and joined the Rosicrucians, a mystical order whose secrets and application of the occult sciences included the prolongation of life, the transmutation of metals and the knowledge of what was happening at a distance. The Brethren were represented by a group of people who had reached high intellectual and occult standards and were the foremost in this field in their day, and it was they who later fostered the notorious Order of the Golden Dawn.

Round about 1838, Lytton himself began to display mystical powers, astonishing all those who witnessed them and amongst which was his ability to move objects at a distance. He also developed considerable skill as an astrologer and was known to make remarkably accurate predictions.

That Lytton was much attracted to the past and its lost worlds is evidenced by his best-known work, *The Last Days of Pompeii*, an interest which again manifested itself in his last book, *The Coming Race*, published just two years before his death in 1873. It concerns a super-race whose earlier existence on Earth, with its collapse of landmasses and natural disasters, had precipitated their underground existence. Possessed of abnormal powers of intellect, they live in immense caverns, hollows and caves beneath the Earth, these townships being linked by subterranean tunnels stretching right round the world.

Much controversy surrounded the publication of this book, described in its blurb as:

'An epic and prophetic Victorian fantasy which explores a civilization beneath the earth where women are masters of men, and masters of a strange force that can destroy, or save, the world.'

It was said that Lytton himself felt uneasy about its publication, the reason being that as he had access to the Rosicrucian secret papers, it was believed that, despite his pledge of secrecy, he had extracted the information he wanted and disguised it in the form of fiction in his unique story.

That *The Coming Race* is much more than fiction is a view held by many authors, amongst them Alec Maclellan, whose own unique book *The Lost World of Agharti* examines the magic of 'Vril-power' and further embraces the reality of the subterranean civilization.

He tells us that the secret knowledge possessed by the

Rosicrucians was believed to have been found in a hidden chamber 'somewhere below ground', and that Lytton, as an occultist, believed in the power of the pentacle as a means of communication. He quotes from Lytton's book *A Strange Story* published in 1861, where he says:

'The pentacle itself has an intelligible meaning, it belongs to the only universal language of symbol, in which all races that think – around and above and below us – can establish communion of thought.'

Alec Maclellan comments:

'If Bulwer Lytton did not actually find a way to the underground world he described in *The Coming Race* – and there is no evidence that he did – might he not have learned something of it through access to ancient knowledge, his mystical powers and the use of the favoured pentacle?'

Maclellan takes the whole concept of underground cities populated by a race who have mastered the control of a fluid force akin to electricity, much further. Based on legend, he pinpoints the underground land known as Agharti as being north of Tibet and with a capital city called Shamballah. He says:

'Taking the legend in its most basic form, Agharti is said to be a mysterious underground kingdom situated somewhere beneath Asia and linked to the other continents of the world by a gigantic network of tunnels. These passageways, partly natural formations and partly the handiwork of the race which created the subterranean nation, provide a means of communication between all the points, and have done so since time immemorial. According to the legend, vast lengths of tunnels still exist today; the rest have been destroyed by cataclysms. The exact location of these passages, and the means of entry, are said to be known only to certain high initiates, and the details are most carefully guarded because the kingdom itself is a vast storehouse of secret knowledge. These manuscripts are claimed to be the works of the lost Atlantean civilization and of an even earlier people who were the first intelligent beings to inhabit the earth.'

His hypothesis is drawn from many different sources, encompassing the origins of the American people, the legend of

Atlantis and the occult secret which Adolf Hitler sought so desperately to appropriate for himself. Even more remarkable is Maclellan's own experience in Yorkshire when he explored a cave whose tunnel sloped gently downwards. Suddenly after walking along it for some time he became aware of a dim glow of light some distance in front of him. He goes on to say:

'Even as I stood there, the light down the tunnel seemed to gain in intensity, although it may only have been an illusion. Cautiously I began to move forward again, the beam of my torch now directed at my feet. I walked carefully, almost holding my breath, for perhaps 50 yards. I could now see that the light was green in colour, and it seemed to be pulsating. Whatever its source was, I had not the faintest idea. I came to a standstill once again.

'Then something even more extraordinary occurred. At first I thought the sound was my own breathing, then I discerned a gentle humming noise that gradually grew louder. As it did so, I felt the ground beneath my feet begin to vibrate, at first ever so gently, but steadily increasing in intensity. The humming became a rumble, and as it did so, the green light appeared to pulsate still more strongly. I felt my heart begin to pound and a sudden terror came over me there in the darkness. *Something* almost seemed to be coming towards me.

'What on Earth was happening? What was the strange light? And what was causing the rumbling beneath my feet? I believed I was in the tunnel of some long forgotten Yorkshire mine, but my senses seemed to be telling me I had stumbled onto something far more extraordinary.'

As the pulsating light and shaking of the ground grew even stronger, Maclellan feared the tunnel would collapse upon him, and he raced back up the passageway, never stopping until he had gained the entrance to the tunnel and, gasping for air, flung himself down on the ground in the sunshine outside. Later, he recounted his experience to some friends who assured him that what he had seen was no illusion, for legend has it that somewhere in the dales of the West Riding of Yorkshire there is an entrance to an underground world. Further research revealed the belief that there exists underneath the old mines at Wharfedale in Yorkshire an underground tunnel that links with others and which ultimately leads to Agharti itself.

In *The Coming Race*, Lytton described '*Vril*-power' as having been used by the inhabitants of Agharti, and says:

'There is no word in any language that I know which is an exact synonym for 'VRIL'. I should call it electricity, except that it comprehends in its manifold branches other forces of nature, to which in our scientific nomenclature, differing names are assigned, such as magnetism, galvanism, etc. These people consider that in 'VRIL' they have arrived at the unity in natural energic agencies, which has been conjectured by many philosophers above ground, and which Faraday (an English experimental physicist who founded the science of electro-magnetism) thus intimates under the more cautious term of correlation: "I have long held an opinion," he says, "almost amounting to a conviction in common with many other lovers of natural knowledge, that the various forms under which the forces of matter are made manifest have one common origin; or, in other words, are so directly related, and mutually dependent, that they are convertible, as it were, into one another, and possess equivalents of power in their action". These subterranean philosophers assert that, by one operation of VRIL, which Faraday would perhaps call "atmospheric magnetism", they can influence the variations of temperature – in plain words, the weather; that by other operations, akin to those ascribed to mesmerism, electro-biology, odic force, etc., but applied scientifically through VRIL conductors, they can exercise influence over minds, and bodies, animal and vegetable, to an extent not surpassed in the romances of our mysticism. To all such agencies they give the common name of VRIL.'

Is 'Vril-power' the manifestation, through a human reactor, of ley power in its purest unfiltered form? It would seem that this could be a distinct possibility on the premise that the source of ley power is mostly, or in part, subterranean. It would appear, therefore, that control of it would give absolute power, and Lytton begins to realise the true ambitions of the underground people, the Vril-ya, when he says in The Coming Race:

'I arrived at the conclusion that this people – though originally not only of our human race, but, as it seems to me clear by the roots of their language, descended from the same ancestors as the great Aryan family, from which in varied streams has flowed the dominant civilisation of the world; and having, according to their myths and their history passed through phases of society familiar to ourselves – had yet now developed into a distinct species with which it was impossible that any community in the upper world could amalgamate. And that if they ever emerged from these nether recesses into the light of day, they

126

would, according to their own traditional persuasions of their ultimate destiny, destroy and replace our existent varieties of man.'

Lytton concludes his amazing fantasy (so-called) with the following warning:

'Only, the more I think of a people calmly developing, in regions excluded from our sight and deemed uninhabitable by our sages, powers surpassing our most disciplined modes of force, and virtues to which our life, social and political, becomes antagonistic in proportion as our civilization advances, – the more devoutly I pray that ages may yet elapse before there emerge into sunlight our inevitable destroyers. Being, however, frankly told by my physician that I am afflicted by a complaint which, though it gives little pain and no perceptible notice of its encroachment, may at any moment be fatal, I have thought it my duty to my fellow-men to place on record these forewarnings of The Coming Race.'

As he himself had only two years to live after his book was published, his words were prophetic in more ways than one. Whatever feelings one may have about *The Coming Race* it nevertheless accurately predicts the development of laser technology and nuclear power, the rise of women, and all the horrific experimentation associated with super-race politics. And, disastrously for Europe and most of the world, one man at least believed so deeply in the existence of '*Vril*-power' and the concept of 'The Coming Race' that he sent expeditions into Asia for the purpose of harnessing the power for himself. That man was Adolf Hitler.

HITLER'S QUEST FOR OCCULT POWER

'I have not come into the world to make men better but to make use of their weaknesses.'
Adolf Hitler

Hitler's Table Talk, 1941–44

The Tibetan Connection
On 25 April 1945 a group of Russian soldiers sifting through the rubble that was Berlin made an astonishing discovery in the

ruins of a three-storey building. In one of the ground floor rooms they found the bodies of seven men, six lying in a circle around the seventh man whose hands were clasped together and encased in bright green gloves. The corpses were all wearing German military uniforms, but they were definitely not Germans.

Whilst the Russian soldiers stared in disbelief, a Mongolian amongst them declared the bodies to be those of Tibetans, and by their precise arrangement it seemed that a ceremonial group suicide had accounted for their bizarre deaths. In the days that followed, more Tibetans were found, some reports saying that as many as a thousand were recorded, all apparently having committed suicide in a similar ritualistic manner.

The discovery of these groups in war-stricken Berlin was to lead to amazing revelations regarding Adolf Hitler's search for occult power and its connection with the underground world of Agharti as well as with Lord Lytton's controversial book, *The Coming Race*. How had it all begun?

Obsession

As is well known, Hitler was emotionally excitable and often easily influenced, especially by people with whom he had a certain rapport. He was also drawn to occultism and the Elementals of the Deva kingdom, contact with which, as mentioned in the previous chapter, Dion Fortune warned could lead a mentally unstable person into obsession, and Hitler certainly seems to be proof of this.

He displayed these obsessive tendencies early on in life, at the age of fifteen, according to August Kubizek, who attended a performance of Wagner's opera *Rienzi* (in which the rise and fall of a Roman tribune is dramatically told) in company with the young Hitler, on whom it had obviously made a profound impression. In discussing it later, Kubizek tells how Hitler gripped his hands in an ecstasy of excitement whilst gazing at him as if mesmerised, and spoke in what seems to have been bursts of an 'elemental force'. 'It was as if another being spoke out of his body,' Kubizek said.

From Kubizek we learn also that Hitler spent a lot of his youth studying occultism which included oriental mysticism, hypnotism and astrology and that he attached great importance to Teutonic mythology. A character in one of Wagner's operas was based on the notorious ninth-century tyrant named Landulph whose pursuit of power had led him to study the black arts, and Hitler apparently identified with him. The works of the philosopher Nietzsche also impressed him – as they had Shelley – especially his teachings that the strong only ought to survive, his works *Evil* and *The Will to Power*, and his doctrine of the superman. With Nietzsche, also, he shared a love of the Wagnerian operas.

By the time he was twenty, Adolf Hitler had met up with another Adolf – Adolf Lanz – who saw fit to change his name to the more impressive one of 'Dr Jorg Lanz von Liebenfels', and who had forsaken his Cistercian monkhood to start a temple dedicated to a new order of the Templars in Werfenstein Castle on the Danube. His followers consisted of a small band of wealthy intellectuals, and Hitler. He performed ritual magic, ran a propaganda magazine devoted to occultism and race mysticism, and the flag proudly flying at the masthead of his rundown castle was a swastika. Hitler, it seems, was his most devout pupil, and he predicted that the young man who followed his every word so avidly would one day be victorious and 'develop a movement that will make the world tremble'. It was from these dark shamanistic beginnings that the fate of millions was decided, but that, as they say, is all history.

The Swastika's Symbolism
The swastika is one of the earliest symbols known, originating probably in Mesopotamia where it has been found on Elamite pottery, but it has also been discovered in India, China, Tibet, Iran, Asia Minor, Etruria, Sweden, Mexico, Peru and Britain. In America it is thought to represent north, south, east and west and to symbolise the ruler of the winds and rain. It has been used on tombs, rock carvings, Celtic stones and coins, is associated with Buddhism and has been used for centuries in Japan as an heraldic cognisance both in its left-hand and right-hand forms.

In Northern Europe it was known as the Hammer of Thor, the Scandinavian god of thunder, which is probably the reason so many English church bells bear the symbol, for in ancient times it was believed the ringing of the bells afforded protection from tempests. Many vestments of sculptural figures bear swastikas, including that of Bishop Edington of Winchester.

It is believed in India that the right-handed swastika is the symbol of Ganesa or Ganupati, master and protector of all auspicious ceremonies and of the sun of the upper world in its daily course. The left-handed or sinister swastika is the symbol of Kali and also the sun of the underground world in its nightly course west to east. The left-handed swastika has always been held to be unlucky, representing as it does everything associated with darkness, and it was this form that was chosen by Adolf Hitler to represent the Third Reich.

It was when the German National Socialist party was still in its infancy in the 1920s that Hitler asked for suggestions to be submitted to him for a sign akin to that of communist Russia's hammer and sickle to represent the German movement, and it was a fellow-occultist named Friedrich Krohn who suggested a black swastika on a white disc with a red background (red for blood, white for nationalism and the purity of race and the swastika for 'the struggle for victory of Aryan man'). Hitler himself had the swastika reversed in what the author Francis King describes as being 'an evocation of evil, spiritual devolution and black magic'.

This action of Hitler's indicated very clearly to Krohn the direction in which he would be leading the country, for, being a member of the *Germanenorden* (German Order) composed mostly of professional men and German officers, he was convinced – as they were – that the Jews were planning a massive conspiracy backed-up by occult practices. (In this connection it is disturbing to note that current racist literature being distributed in this country warns similarly of 'the destruction of our Celtic Anglo-Saxon race by Mongrelisation' planned by 'International Jewry headed by Jewish money barons and backed up by occult secret societies'.)

Krohn endeavoured to counter this supposed Jewish uprising in Germany by establishing an occult-based new Nordic society of freemasonry. At their elaborate rituals members wore Viking helmets and robes and wielded swords, the organisation being called the Thule Society, the name having been derived from a fabled land similar to Paradise. Members were recruited from many walks of life including those drawn from the lower classes, and the Society's various newspapers spread copious anti-Semitic material, one of which – the *Volkischer Beobachter* – was eventually adopted by the Nazi Party as their official journal. But of all the occultists whom Hitler knew and who helped to shape his destiny, perhaps the one who influenced him the most was a man called Karl Haushofer.

The Nazis' Master Magician

Born in Bavaria in 1869, Karl Haushofer came from a wealthy military background. A man of high intellect, he was educated at Munich University after which he, not surprisingly, joined the German army. It was during this period that he developed a deep interest in mysticism and gained further occult knowledge when his army duty took him to the Far East. In their book *The Morning of the Magicians*, Louis Pauwels and Jacques Bergier say that Haushofer made several visits to India and the Far East and that when he was sent to Japan he learned Japanese. The authors go on to say:

'He believed that the German people originated in Central Asia, and that it was the Indo-Germanic race that guaranteed the permanence, nobility and greatness of the world. While in Japan, Haushofer is said to have been initiated into one of the most important secret Buddhist societies and to have sworn, if he failed in his 'mission', to commit suicide in accordance with the time-honoured ceremonial.'

Among his many accomplishments, Haushofer acquired that of prophecy, which he carried out with consummate skill and uncanny precision, accurately predicting where enemy bombs would drop and shells would fire during World War 1. Whilst this alarmed both his men and his superiors, his stature increased enormously.

Haushofer attained the rank of General – one of the youngest men to have done so – and after the war was over he returned to Munich University, gained a Doctorate in political geography and began teaching the subject he had himself created called 'The Science of Geo-Politics'. This fusion of geography and politics derived from an original idea developed by Sir Halford John Mackinder (1861–1947) a Scotsman who wrote of the value of geography as a factor in social reconstruction, to which Haushofer added his own nationalistic beliefs, instilling into his new students that it was the destiny of the German people to one day rule Europe and Asia, the homeland of the Aryan people. He considered that Central Asia was the heartland from which the Indo-Germanic master race had emerged, and therefore Germany must recover it and thereby exercise their right for world control which only they were fitted to administer.

In the *Geo-Political Review*, journal of the Institute for Geo-Politics which Haushofer started, he further expounded his views on Aryan supremacy, revealing that during his travels in Asia he had learned of a race of supermen who dwelt in a vast underground encampment beneath the Himalayas. The place was called Agharti and its capital city was Shamballah.

One of the young men who avidly assimilated the doctrines of Professor Haushofer was Rudolf Hess, who became his assistant at the university and was later to be the fateful link between his Professor and his Führer. It was while Hitler and Hess were in Lansberg Prison in 1924 where they had been incarcerated for their part in the conspiracy to overthrow the Bavarian government, that Hess introduced the two men, and Haushofer visited Hitler every day, according to authors Louis Pauwels and Jacques Bergier, and

'spent hours with him expounding his theories and deducing from them every possible argument in favour of political conquest. Left alone with Hess, Hitler amalgamated, for the purposes of propaganda, the theories of Haushofer, as the basis of *Mein Kampf*.'

Haushofer's influence on Hitler is further confirmed by Edmund A. Walsh in his book *Total Power*, where he writes:

'One can almost feel the presence of Haushofer, although the lines were written by Hess at the dictation of Hitler. What Haushofer did was to hand a sheathed sword of conquest from his arsenal of scholarly research. Hitler unsheathed the blade, sharpened the edge, and threw away the scabbard.'

Hess knew Haushofer perhaps better than anyone, and according to Jack Fishman in his *The Seven Men of Spandau*, it was the former deputy Führer, Rudolf Hess, who revealed that his one-time Professor had been 'the secret Master Magician of the Reich – the power behind Hitler.' Amongst the many books that Haushofer lent Hess was Lytton's *The Coming Race*. Like Lytton, Haushofer had been a member of the Rosicrucians (in a German lodge), and saw Lytton's book as confirmation of his own discoveries about the existence of Agharti. He also thought that the Rosicrucian secrets thus divulged had been well hidden by Lytton in the form of fiction.

Haushofer was instrumental in launching 'a weird society' by the name of 'The Luminous Lodge of the *Vril* Society', the sole aim of which, according to Trevor Ravenscroft in his *The Spear of Destiny* was:

'to make further researches into the origins of the Aryan Race and the manner in which magical capacities slumbering in the Aryan blood could be reactivated to become the vehicle of superhuman powers.'

Mr Ravenscroft goes on to say that the source of inspiration for this was *The Coming Race* by Bulwer Lytton, who

'had no idea that this book, in which he described the emergence of a new race with lofty spiritual faculties and superhuman powers, would become the evil inspiration of a small group of Nazis intent on breeding a Master Race in order to enslave the world.'

In an essay published in 1947 entitled *Pseudo-Sciences Under the Nazi Regime*, Dr Willy Ley, a scientist who had exiled himself from Germany in 1933, said that a number of Tibetan lamas had been recruited into this Lodge because of their association with Agharti, and the members believed they had thus acquired the secret knowledge that would enable them to ultimately become the equals of the underground race. Not only had they developed certain methods of concentration but also 'a whole system of internal gymnastics by which they could be transformed', Dr Ley said.

Most of the Tibetan high lamas who had been brought to Berlin – led by a supremo known only as the Man with Green Gloves – were known intimately to Haushofer, and every time he consulted with Hitler he took along with him the Man with Green Gloves who remained close to the centre of the Nazi elite until the fall of Berlin, and his bizarre death with his fellow countrymen. Had Haushofer, through his close relationship with this mysterious man, acquired the secret of '*Vril*-power'? As he was apparently the prime mover in the 'Luminous Lodge of the *Vril* Society' there are many who believed he had, although it is unlikely he would have been able to have kept it to himself – he was too close to Hitler. In fact, this sinister and highly influential man was believed to be the power behind Hitler, and it is believed that his fashionable, Geo-Political teachings were a cover for his true ambition for the German people. Trevor Ravenscroft says of him in *The Spear of Destiny*:

'He clothed geography in a veil of racial mysticism, providing a reason for the Germans to return to those areas in the hinterland of Asia from which it was generally believed the Aryan Race originated. In this subtle way he incited the German nation towards the conquest of the whole of Eastern Europe and beyond to the vast inner area of Asia which extends 2,500 miles from west to east between the Volga and the Yangtze rivers and includes in its most southerly aspect the mountains of Tibet. It was Haushofer's opinion that whoever gained complete control of this heartland, developed its economic resources and organised its military defence, would achieve unassailable world supremacy.'

It was to this end that – as early as 1926, some reports say – adepts of the inner circle of Nazism organised expeditions to Tibet for the purpose of bringing back those lamas possessed of high occult powers. Trevor Ravenscroft goes on to say:

'Agharti was regarded as a 'Luciferic' headquarters concerned with astral projection and thought-control, Shamballah was an 'Ahrimanic' one exerting power over material nature. Both, it was believed, could provide the means for sowing confusion among inferior races. Nazi emissaries made contact with their governing Orders, but only the Luciferic party proved willing to support Nazism. The Tibetans who came to Germany belonged to this group and were known as the Society of Green Men. They were joined by seven members of the Green Dragon Society of Japan – presumably the group Haushofer belonged to. Instructed by him, the Tibetans were employed by Himmler to teach occultism to the Nazi elite. Agharti and Shamballah were mentioned in testimony at the Nuremberg War Crimes Trials, but nobody understood what the witnesses were talking about.'

Haushofer committed suicide in the ceremonial Japanese manner in 1946 in accordance with his vow, his 'mission' having obviously failed. But did his secrets die with him, or did he communicate them to someone else?

It will be recalled that Rudolf Hess was his confidant for many years, and indeed it is thought that it was Haushofer's dream in which he saw Hess 'striding through the tapestried halls of English castles, bringing peace between the two great Nordic nations' that prompted Hess's ill-fated flight to England in 1941. He actually embarked upon this lunatic mission armed only with a magical Tibetan amulet, and with no possibility of returning to the Fatherland. But in all their long years of friendship it seems reasonable to suppose that Haushofer conveyed at least some of his immense store of occult knowledge to Rudolf Hess, over whom, as we have seen, he held so much influence. How much of the secret of 'Vril-power' did he impart to him? Only Hess himself knows ...

The Cone of Power

Hitler's extraordinary hypnotic powers and his ability to influence others were demonstrated time and again during his reign as Führer, being remarked upon by all who met him. In fact the commander of the U-boat fleet, Karl Donitz, was known to avoid meeting Hitler whenever he could because he said he felt the Führer's 'powers of suggestion' impaired his judgement.

Hitler's ability, during his speeches, to mesmerise the masses was never more apparent than at the huge Nuremberg rallies, the immense gatherings fulfilling the conditions necessary for what is known by many white witches as the 'cone of power'. The idea – developed by Karl Haushofer – required the careful placing of searchlights piercing the night sky so that they formed a conical pattern over Hitler and the masses. The surge of emotion generated by the people's enthusiasm would travel up the cone in waves, to be directed down at its centre onto the ranting and gesticulating figure of Hitler, and fed back into the crowd with immense force.

The basic idea, when used by white witches, is to direct the psychic energy within the cone of spotlights or searchlights towards purely social ends, but Karl Haushofer adapted certain aspects of it so that it became a far more sinister cycle of force, and was used by Hitler with devastating success. The Nuremberg rallies remain on record as a frightening monument to the success of the interaction between one man and a vast assembled crowd over which he held complete control.

This, amongst other things, has led many occultists to believe that by that time (1938) Hitler had become a powerful black magician in his own right, and although Josef Goebbels, his propaganda minister, did not share his belief in the occult, one man who did was the notorious Heinrich Himmler.

Born of middle-class parents in Munich in 1900, Himmler was an inconspicuous, weak-looking youth who abandoned his Catholic upbringing for occultism while still in his teens. Described by occult writer J.H. Brennan as 'a zombie without mind or soul of its own', Himmler was nevertheless made Deputy Reichsführer of the SS – the *Schutzstaffel* – while it was still only a force of some 300 men, but by 1933 he had built it up to such strength that he was able to purge its membership of all those unable to prove a non-Jewish ancestry as far back as 1750.

Believing himself to be the reincarnation of the founder of the Saxon royal house, who died in 936, Himmler devised a specific SS religious ceremony derived from his worship of Woden and embodying neo-pagan and occult elements, which his men were obliged to attend. He also devised new festivals to replace those of Christmas and Easter, and scrapped baptism and marriage ceremonies, saying that polygamy would best serve the interests of the elite SS guards. At the same time, he incorporated in his instructions to them such bizarre orders as the correct way of committing suicide.

In view of the fact that those at the very centre of the Nazi Party were deeply involved in occult practices, it seems incongruous that they issued a directive in 1934 forbidding any type of occultism, including such relatively harmless pursuits as palmistry, astrology, and fortune-telling, to be practised any-where in Germany. They also put a ban on all writers of occult subjects, and this included von Liebenfels, who had been such an influence on Hitler during his early years before Hess had introduced Hitler to Haushofer, but who was consequently forbidden to publish any more books on magic. This suppression of all occult groups also included the German Order and the Thule Society, to the amazement of its members, many of whom were Nazis. By 1940, the ban was extended to all German-occupied countries, occultists of whatever persuasion being either destroyed or driven underground.

This left the inner circle of the Nazi Party – and in particular the Triad composed of Hitler as supreme magus, Himmler as his acolyte and Haushofer as the master guru – the sole practitioners of the black arts in Germany. By banning all other occultists they were able to pursue their own perverted practices unhampered by possible interference from any other occult movement. But this sort of ploy could not, of course, have any lasting, or wider, effect, and it is said that Britain's white witches combined together to successfully combat Hitler's evil intentions – especially when it seemed evident that a German invasion was imminent.

Despite his defeat in 1945, Hitler's pact with the 'powers of darkness' lasted to the very end, for he delayed shooting himself until the 30 April – *Walpurgisnacht* – the notorious Sabbat of the black witches, who claim that all children born on that day belong to the devil. Did Hitler think, in his twisted mind, that by dying on that particular day he was ensuring his own regeneration?

Hitler's pursuit of power was short-lived in relation to the Thousand Year Reich which he intended to be ruled by the master race, and lacking in detailed information, but is there, somewhere in the archives, documentation of his hopeless occult quest? If so, is it now in the hands of the Russians?

One man who might provide the answers to such questions is the sole inhabitant of Spandau Prison, Rudolf Hess, for not only was he in the confidence of Haushofer but he was also present on the many occasions that Hitler and Haushofer held their most secret meetings. He must therefore have witnessed much of what transpired at those meetings, and have known how far Haushofer and Hitler had got with their pursuit of '*Vril*-power'.

Can it be that that knowledge has been gradually extracted by the Russians during all Hess's years of imprisonment? Constantly watched and guarded by the Russians, Hess is not even allowed to see any reference to the Nazi era, either through his personal mail or via the media. Why is this?

It is known that the Russians have also been experimenting with the paranormal in recent years. Is this why they refuse so vehemently to release Hess, frail and ageing though he is? Are they afraid that he knows too much?

11 *THE DEMONIC CONNECTION – THE WIDER IMPLICATIONS*

'We will select other areas in which to spread the word.'
Initiate of *The Friends of Hecate*
during a secret meeting with Charles Walker, 1978

THE KGB's PARAPSYCHOLOGY PROGRAMME

'Our programme includes the propaganda of atheism.'
Lenin

Mind Games – The Serious Side

From the time the scientist Vladimir Bekhterev launched the Commission for the Study of Mental Suggestion in Leningrad in 1922, Russia has been secretly involved in experiments concerning the study of thought transference. Over the years their investigation into parapsychology has expanded rapidly to include all aspects of mind power and mind control, with many distinguished scientists joining forces with mediums and other sensitives in a programme of mind games which even Joseph Stalin took an interest in at one time. Since then they have come a long way, being deadly serious in their pursuit of all things appertaining to mind control. But it took two forward thinking Americans, Lynn Schroeder and Sheila Ostrander, to brave the ridicule of the Western Press and publish a book entitled *Psychic Discoveries Behind the Iron Curtain*, which, while arousing merely sceptical curiosity in the West, drew a vitriolic outburst from the Soviets. The book 'overflows with factual errors and undisguised anti-Soviet thrusts' was one comment, which served the more to confirm to the Americans the two authors' integrity. Perhaps the real reason behind the Russian anger was the fact that too many secrets had been given away by the scientist – Eduard Naumov – who had assisted the women with the writing of the book, in which it was disclosed that the Russian military had been experimenting with telepathic communication between shore and submarines and that a method had been discovered whereby such a telepathic signal could be 'jammed'. Experimentation of this nature clearly indicated that the USSR was considering paranormal powers to be a potential weapon of war.

In 1973, Chairman Leonid Brezhnev called for a global ban on a weapon 'more terrifying than nuclear weaponry', and although he did not enlarge on his words it was assumed at the time that the USA knew what he meant, especially as Eduard Naumov was serving a sentence in a forced labour camp for 'political disruption' following his part in the publication in 1970 of the American authors' book.

During the years 1972–5, reports were prepared for the US Defense Intelligence Agency under the umbrella title of 'Soviet and Czechoslovak Para-Psychology Research', and contained such words and phrases as: 'astral espionage' and 'thought conditioning', together with the envisaged effects of their application. Extra funds were made available in the US for research into the paranormal, and one of the best works to appear on the subject came from Lieutenant Colonel J.B. Alexander in his article entitled *The New Mental Battlefield*, published in a US Army journal, in which he said that although many people would find the concept unacceptable 'since it does not conform to their ideas of reality', the nations of the world should take a serious interest in the paranormal in the light of the Soviet involvement.

Sinister 'Woodpecker'

In 1976, a Russian radio station at Gomel, near Minsk, was discovered to be transmitting a powerful signal that was interfering with television, conventional radio, telegraph message, and even close-call telephone systems. The signal, known as 'Woodpecker' because of its chattering character, was beamed across the globe twenty-four hours a day, seven days a week. Many countries complained, and in due course the Russians apologised whilst not offering any feasible explanation for their behaviour, but after an eighteen month period the transmissions gradually weakened and finally stopped in 1978. But not, it seems, before a sinister purpose behind 'Woodpecker' was revealed. In 1977, an American paranormal investigator by the name of Andrija Puharich demonstrated to a startled London audience that the broadcasts were a giant stationary wave that passed through the Earth in tune with the natural vibrations of the atmosphere. This wave, which was of extremely low frequency – the ELF band – acted directly upon the human brain's subliminal impulses, i.e. those which deal with involuntary control. Extensive exposure to ELF waves has been proved by tests to bring about abnormal tiredness and irritability and also render the subject more conducive to suggestions from an outside source.

This frightening control of the human mind was foreseen by Eldon Byrd, an engineer, scientist and warfare analyst employed in America's Naval Surface Weapons Center, who in 1981 maintained that human behaviour could be affected from a distance by 'electrical entrainment of the firing rate of nerve tissue in the brain'. He warned then that 'The Soviets are investigating exotic technologies – involving in part the use of electromagnetic signals to alter behaviour – that are virtually ignored in the Western world.'

Mr Byrd also warns that if the Russians are able to perfect such technologies, the whole of the Western world would be caught by surprise and have little in the way of counter measures. But he predicts that if the danger is recognised in time, such technologies can indeed be countered. He also foresees the new scientific discovery of weapons of war being based on forms of energy transfer other than that deriving from a chemical explosion or a nuclear effect, and that 'the laws of physics will have to be extended and expanded into other dimensions to accommodate the discoveries'.

Whether or not he was referring to the experiment aboard the *Eldridge* is not of course known, but he goes on to say that 'the impact will be as profound as the jump from Newton's macrophysical laws to quantum mechanics'. Has that 'jump' already occurred – in Russia?

Instrument for Coercion
In 1917, Lenin said, 'The state is an instrument for coercion', and in his book *KGB*, Brian Freemantle says,

'After 65 years, the KGB have become that instrument. The parapsychology experiments are the ultimate in the KGB attempts to control the minds of the people.'

A former foreign correspondent and foreign editor of the London *Daily Mail*, Mr Freemantle makes an in-depth study of Russia's use of parapsychology as a weapon.

He tells us that since 1960, the Soviet Union has opened seven new laboratories to study parapsychology and that it is believed by intelligence experts in the West that they have already developed an instrument which is capable of measuring the electrical signals emitted from the brain. At Novosibirsk, where it is known that KGB scientists are experimenting in germ warfare, a Special Department 8, working under the aegis of the Soviet Academy of Science, is conducting experiments in 'thought transference' with remarkable success. Exiled Soviet scientist August Stern, now in the USA, worked for three years in Novosibirsk on experiments carried out to find a physical basis for psychic energy, known as 'Psi particles', and in Leningrad and Moscow both military and naval scientists are researching the enigma of thought transference.

The man considered to be the foremost Soviet scientist in the field of parapsychology is I.M. Kogan, director of the GRU (Gosurdarstarvenoi Razvedyvatelnaya, the State Military Information Agency)-controlled laboratory in the Soviet Scientific Technical Society of Radiotechnique and Electrocommunication. Together with another leader in this field, a man named Gennadii Aleksandrovich Sergeyev, Kogan is working on the theory that mental telepathy is possible through the medium of electromagnetic radiation, and experiments and training sessions are being conducted along these lines.

At the Leningrad Institute for Brain Research, the KGB are showing great interest in the research of scientist L.L. Vasiliev who is attempting to use telepathy over a long distance in order to influence people. Kogan is also engaged in similar long-distance mental communication, and all the laboratories for parapsychological experimentation are engaged in conducting automatic hypnosis. With this particular experiment, scientists have devised a 'remote-controlled therapeutic apparatus' code-named 'Lida' which emits pulsating light, heat and sound on VHF.

In 1977, Robert Toth, correspondent of the *Los Angeles Times*, was arrested, jailed and then expelled from the Soviet Union for writing about the Russian interest in parapsychology, he having been accused of 'receiving state secrets'. It is consequently believed by scientists attached to intelligence sources in the West that the Soviet research is directed more specifically towards intelligence uses. The French in particular are of the opinion that the Russians are experimenting with parapsychology for the purposes of surveillance, espionage and thought control.

Noxious Effects

Since the mid-1970s, the Americans have claimed, although it has not been proven, that the Russians have been directing micro-electric waves at their embassy in Moscow in the form of two beams being emitted from separate sites either side of the US embassy building. They had, in fact, installed their own equipment for monitoring the beams.

On the 20 January 1979, the *Daily Telegraph* carried a report of a fire which had swept through a Moscow building 'from which American diplomats believe radiation is being directed against the US embassy'. When embassy officials switched on their monitoring equipment after the fire, it was found that no signal was coming from the fire-damaged building, and only a very weak one from the other building that they maintained the Russians were sending a signal from, but despite this proof, the Russians denied any knowledge of the matter.

During the 1975–85 period it appears that staff at the US embassy suffered from more than the average amount of illnesses, these including the inexplicable development of blood disorders and many cases of stress-related illnesses including severe depression. This high incidence of illness is thought to be a direct result of the Russians' bombardment of the embassy by radio waves.

If this is so, it not only emphasises the rapid advances which have been made in this new and frightening field of mind experimentation, but it also highlights the utter inability of those against whom it is directed to protect themselves in any way. Mind control is more than a two-edged sword: it is a multi-purpose weapon of war against which, at the present time, there seems to be no antidote.

Where, in all this mounting evidence, does an advanced elitist group such as the Friends of Hecate, fit in?

THE BREAKDOWN OF SOCIETY

'The worst difficulties from which we suffer do not come from without. They come from within. They do not come from the cottages of the wage-earners. They come from a peculiar type of brainy people always found in our country, who, if they add something to its culture, take much from its strength.'

Winston Churchill
Speech on St George's Day, London, 1933

Intellectual Leeches

Strength is being taken from Britain now. It is being drained by power-hungry intellectuals who form elite groups and secret societies and who use their clandestine organisations in furtherance of their own avowed aims.

Some groups masquerade behind patriotic-sounding names; others identify with a relevant historical character from the past, while those practising occultism usually base their cults on demonic or mythical deities. Few advertise either their existence or their cause; most adhere to secret selective enrolment, and all appeal – initially at least – to specific and in some cases, the debased requirements of their group, which may involve physical and psychological violence. Most are constitutionally parasitical, and where demonic groups are concerned, feed off the people in some way or another. With a group as occultly advanced as the Friends of Hecate appear to be, it is the psychic energies of the ordinary people and those holding higher office that are being drained and manipulated.

As has been suggested the immense power carried by the leys is akin to the life force of the planet itself, and anyone able to tap, direct and control this force has a very powerful influence at their fingertips – an influence which, in the wrong hands, could be used, to disrupt and break down society, without society realising what was happening.

This latent occult power, known to the ancients and revered by the seers and magicians of former times, has been greatly sought after down the ages. But when it is corrupted through a combination of ritual black magic and Satanism in its most

143

malignant form, its scientific projection could lead to national disaster. With an organisation of several hundred elite 'inner core' members and many thousands of underlings holding rituals at sites throughout the British Isles, the aims of this advanced secret cult could indeed be far-reaching – catastrophic, even. In fact, its influence is already being felt in this country today, for if, as seems probable, this cult is sending out and directing a type of negative thought force which is capable of tampering telepathically with the brain and altering human behaviour patterns, such altered states of behaviour may have been manifesting themselves during the past ten years or so. What evidence is there of this?

One of the most disturbing patterns to emerge in recent years concerns the incidence of suicides among young people. The negativism of these youthful 'no-hopers' can be exacerbated psychically while the mind is temporarily weakened by disturbed emotions, overstudying, unhappy relationships, alcoholism or drug addiction. Statistics show that whereas in 1975 the number of young people under the age of twenty-four who had killed themselves amounted to 169, in 1983 the number had more than doubled to 372 suicides. In view of the fact that for every successful attempt there are about 50 which fail, on this premise alone we arrive at the alarming figure of over 18,000 young people whose thinking and attitudes are annually being so harmfully influenced that they can visualise no future for themselves and so seek to end their own lives.

Negativism, the soil of social indifference in which the obnoxious weeds of demonic cults and extremist groups thrive, spreads itself like a cancer into every section of our communities.

Another instance of organised occult disruption could be the so-called football hooliganism which has spread and assumed alarming proportions during the past ten years, culminating in 1985 in Brussels at the European Cup Final where the violence far exceeded anything previously witnessed at occasions such as this and which had little to do with our national game. Thoroughly scrutinised videos of the incident revealed the presence of some members of an extreme right wing Italian group known to the police, among the spectators. Several members of far-right British parties were also present, and as they were dressed up as Liverpool supporters, it was felt by many that they actually started the riot. Was this therefore a planned programme of violence especially for this event?

The escalation of violence generally, especially among young offenders, the increase in crime, terrorist activity and riots – which have become the new negative social phenomenon of our time – all thrust deeply into the core of our inner cities, thus striking at the very heart of society. Do they 'just happen', or are they planned, psychically backed-up and physically carried out as part of a much larger programme of disruption?

It is relatively easy to fuel the genuine anger of people who are out on the edge of society and to provoke a gut reaction to unemployment, police oppression and racism by riot. Consequently, the authorities pass legislation that is seen to limit the rights of individuals. With counteractive measures continuing to be taken in this way, confrontation is exacerbated. The situation can therefore soon lead to a more general destabilisation, and the total breakdown that groups like the Friends of Hecate are seeking.

Details of the Satanic cults' aims against society have been uncovered by the Christian Exorcism Study Group which has been gathering information mainly from defecting Satanists but also from other cult members. Its report gives some chilling findings. General secretary Paul Sturgess believes there are 8 major Satanic and other occult organisations operating in Britain today, all of which have extensive international links. There are an estimated 30,000 people belonging to these various organisations, 7,000 pertaining to OTO (Ordo Templi Orientis) which is the largest group based in West Hampstead, London.

The Study Group reports that many organisations change their names and use different ones so that total security is maintained. Is it possible, therefore, that the Friends of Hecate and the OTO are affiliated? Their aims are similar. According to the Study Group, the aims of these organisations is 'to corrupt society and overturn the order of things', and they believe that Satanists are involved in some of the more extreme Left- and Right-wing political groups.

It is suspected that the Friends of Hecate are using members of suitable extremist political groups for the practical purpose of violent persuasion in pursuance of their own destructive aims against society. All the evidence is there, and if they are indeed the instigators of a programme of destabilization in Britain, how advanced are they in implementing it, and when is it designed to culminate in the orgy of nationwide chaos they seem to be striving to attain? Perhaps the answer can be deduced, in part, from our knowledge of other extremist groups with which there are possible connections.

Modern Extremist Factions

In his compelling book entitled *Left-Right* concerning the march of political extremism in Britain, the former Labour MP for Meriden, Mr John Tomlinson, has chronicled the ideas and activities of groups which occupy the outer fringes of the political spectrum. One group in particular which is relevant to our subject is called 'The League of Saint George', which, cloaked under the name of a folk hero and saint implying patriotism, is nevertheless deemed by Mr Tomlinson to be one of the most sinister of the far-right organisations in Britain today.

Formed in 1974 from a breakaway group of disgruntled members of the Union Movement who had found Sir Oswald Mosley's anti-Semitic views too moderate for their liking, the League now boasts nationwide membership which is mainly composed of people drawn from the professions and those of the middle classes. Their internal organisation seems to be tiered much in the same way as the spiral leading to the elite inner circle of occult groups whereby only those attaining this highest level of office are entrusted with the League's operational and other secrets. Their leadership is composed of a select group of persons fully experienced in all aspects of extremism and the copious literature it produces includes both Nazi and racist material.

In fact, the League considers itself to be a superior order of Nazi, officially being seen to despise the street fighting type of thuggery displayed by organisations such as the National Front and the British Movement whilst at the same time having no scruples about infiltrating these other groups for the express purpose of influencing their policies and recruiting suitable members for themselves.

The League is also involved in Odinism, a worship based on the Norse god of war, with a blend of both Nordic and Celtic mythology. 'Odinism', Mr Tomlinson says, 'is a practice both occult and fear-inducing.' This 'order through fear' has its adherents in most extremist groups and is a doctrine to which ultra-right-wing organisations in particular are dedicated. Amongst its promotional publications, the Odinist Committee of London's *Raven Banner* maintains that this primitive and superstitious form of paganism represents 'a return to the heroic idealistic philosophy of our age'.

Describing itself as a 'non-party, non-sectarian political club', the League ranges itself firmly against the threat of Communism. It is dedicated to the spread of National Socialist ideology calculated by its activities to achieve a European Union of 'nationalists', and to this end, in addition to the spreading of National Socialist propaganda, the League co-ordinates with other sympathetic groups including the British fascists, and acts overall as an 'umbrella organisation servicing the fascist movement'.

Members regularly attend paramilitary training and briefing held in secret at camps throughout the country where they work together with other extremist groups. In addition to celebrating Hitler's birthday, they also honour the memory of Nazi collaborators and co-ordinate the British fascist's annual pilgrimage to Diksmuide in Belgium, an excursion which attracts Nazis from throughout Europe as well as from farther afield.

The rally held there in the summer of 1980 was reported to have been particularly well attended by British Nazi contingents, and in addition to the usual marches and traditional parades that took place, it is believed there was a top-level secret meeting between British and European paramilitary groups concerning future strategy. John Tomlinson thinks it possible that the bomb outrages carried out subsequently in Bologna, Munich and Paris in which a hundred people lost their lives, may well have been co-ordinated at that Diksmuide meeting. The Italian police, however, were of the opinion that the bombings – specifically the Bologna outrage – could have been masterminded by the Masonic P2 Lodge. The scandal surrounding this outlawed Masonic Lodge broke in 1981, and because Italian police investigations implicated so many senior politicians and public figures, it caused the downfall of Premier Forlani's government that same year.

The Grand Master of the P2 Lodge was Licio Gelli, who has been wanted since 1982 for alleged fraud and corruption involving over £70 million. Although he was captured he disappeared from his cell in Geneva in 1983 whilst waiting for extradition to Italy. A hypodermic needle with traces of blood was found in his cell and Swiss officials believe he was kidnapped.

A close colleague of Gelli's was the President of the Ambrosiano Bank, Robert Calvi, known as 'God's Banker' because many Vatican priests were paid through it. Robert Calvi was found hanged beneath Blackfriars Bridge on the Thames in London in June 1982.

It is thought by Interpol that the Masonic P2 Lodge was involved in international arms deals, drug trafficking, blackmail and extortion, and they also believe that the P2s used terrorists from both the Left and Right in order to implement a programme of destabilisation in Italy for the purpose of installing and maintaining a strong, right-wing government.

Much of the Masonic P2 Lodge's funding was said to have come from Lodges and similarly affiliated right-wing groups in the United States of America. The League of Saint George also has strong links with America, its principal contacts there being the Ku Klux Klan and the National States Rights Party, and it has 'understandings' with neo-nazi groups stretching across the globe: Canada, the USA, Argentina, Australia, New Zealand, South Africa, Holland, France and every country in Western Europe. The League also recruits for – and screens – the highly secretive Column 88, which includes many of its own top members.

Formed in 1970, this paramilitary group's name derives from the eighth letter of the alphabet, being HH for *Heil Hitler*, and its recruitment, membership and business are held in the highest secrecy. Would-be recruits are required to have reached a high standard in many subversive areas including intelligence work and the technicalities of handling arms and explosives. Their specialised training includes guerrilla warfare, and it is suspected that they have already infiltrated the Volunteer Reserve of the Territorial Army and established contact with the regular Army. It also seems probable that this highly organised and highly secret group has contacts with active terrorist units in both Italy and Palestine through which Arab funding is received to augment the financial assistance it receives from wealthy Nazi parties in Europe.

When recruits are accepted they are allotted to individual cells, their orders and information henceforth being relayed to them through tape recordings, a method used by commanders and prime movers in most subversive organisations to link cells nationally while maintaining absolute secrecy. In this way, orders are given without the need of ever having to divulge the identities of the commanders and 'top brass' involved.

Like the League of Saint George, Column 88 members are devotees of occultism, Nordic/Celtic-based deific worship, and the concept of racial purity. The anti-fascist journal *Searchlight* claims that the ambition of Column 88 is:

'to have their members in places of influence across the whole spectrum of the Right from Monday Club to the National Front, and to slowly but surely make sure that National Socialism is not only not forgotten but also edges ahead bit by bit within these groups.'

A group similar to both the League of Saint George and Column 88 is known as SS Wotan 18, which shares the occult beliefs of the other two but is even more ominous in that it is said to have its own considerable stockpile of arms which, amongst other sophisticated weaponry, includes anti-tank guns and grenades.

Perhaps one of the most distressing aspects of extremist activity is the way in which children are increasingly becoming involved. Schools are already targets for recruitment into the National Front and the left-wing Socialist Workers' Party, and Mr Tomlinson believes that the British Movement and the Militant Tendency are also now turning their attention to this arena. In fact, worried Labour Party officials in Swansea have discovered that this is already happening in their area. One parent whose 14-year-old daughter was recruited by Militant said that they were as fanatical as the Moonies religious cult. The recruitments came to light when Militant presented local Labour councillors with 15 signed-up new membership forms, and when the Labour Party officials called at the houses to meet their new members personally, they discovered they were all school children.

The parents of one girl – themselves lifelong Labour supporters – said that Militant were just like Hitler 'trying to get people as young as they can in order to fill their minds with extremist doctrines'.

Mr Chris Gaine, lecturer in multi-racial education at a West

Sussex Institute of Higher Education, maintains that in West Sussex 50 per cent of pupils are racially prejudiced and that school children displayed open hostility to other races. In a survey of essays written by 12-year-olds, half were abusive about coloured people and Mr Gaine thought that the lives of future generations would be distorted by racism unless the prejudices of today's children were corrected.

But it is not only the extremist groups that are infiltrating our schools, for many new cults are springing up like mushrooms throughout the democratic world, and their specific target is children and young people.

Scourge of the Cults

Over the past ten years, cult-power has become a menacing reality, sucking into its insatiable maw the most idealistic and sensitive types of youngster, those ready and willing to involve themselves wholeheartedly in any cause, cult or cadre which says its aims are the enrichment of individual life and the betterment of the world.

It is estimated that in Britain today there are as many as 300 cults such as the Moonies, Rajneesh and the Jesus Fellowship with a total membership of anything up to 20,000 impressionable young people comprised of teenagers and young adults, all of whom have sworn allegiance to their particular cult and who are so mentally conditioned by its doctrines that every aspect of their lives is disciplined to the exclusion of their personal desires. This absolute obedience embraces even the major issues of the members' lives, such as career choice and marriage plans, and by playing on the hackneyed 'generation gap' often divides families.

As with the groups based on political extremism, many of these new-found cults parade under a religious banner or are geared to some remote Eastern philosophy appealing more specifically to the spiritual needs of the less materialistic member. According to the Christian Exorcism Study Group, many Satanists operate under the cover of legitimate organisations of a theosophical or transcendental nature. But all seem to have a crusading ring about them calculated to intrigue and tempt would-be members.

Another point of similarity with extremist groups is the secrecy which surrounds the exact aims of the cult, which many disciples do not discover until they are well and truly involved in its activities. Some then find themselves too physically restricted – if not actually held – by the confines of the cult, to leave; others become psychologically disturbed by its doctrines so that they see parents and family as enemies, and the cult as their only true means of liberation, whilst yet others are so skilfully manipulated that their minds are virtually under the control of the charismatic cult leader or guru, thus rendering them unwilling or unable to break away. In fact where these unfortunate members are concerned, an escape can only be engineered with outside help, which, in the case of those over the age of eighteen, is tantamount to abduction. At any rate, without the consent of the member concerned, which is rarely if ever forthcoming, such a 'kidnapping' could be legally construed as such by the cult's hierarchy. Even where parents have made a successful attempt to reclaim an offspring in this way, his or her thinking processes have been so completely manipulated that a rigorous course of post-cultic de-programming supervised by experts in this particular field of mental rehabilitation is vital before a normal life-style is regained.

The whole harmful concept of these demanding cults is a thinly-disguised 'order through fear' dictum, similar to that instilled in members of an occult-based extremist group. A willingness to serve, conformity, and dedication to what members are *persuaded to think* is a good cause, become the way of life and very existence of the members. Trading on the gullibility of youth, such cults, which operate behind a screen of ambiguity, are becoming a very real menace in today's society, and of all the multifarious cults making a bid for control over the world's youth, those demonically-based pose the greatest threat.

In Monroe, Michigan, USA, a seventeen-year-old youth who was found murdered on the 2 February 1986 is believed to have been the victim of a sacrificial killing by devil-worshippers who were celebrating the witches' Sabbat of Candlemas.

Police Chief Michael Davidson said that after a two-week investigation during which students at three high schools were questioned, he and his detectives were convinced that the youth had been killed during a sacrificial ceremony.

'We have uncovered what appears to be several rings of devil-worshippers in the town among teenagers', he said, according

151

to a report in the *Daily Express* of the 22 February 1986, 'and the youth's killing was definitely connected to one of them.'

The youth, whose name was Lloyd Gamble, was found dead in an outbuilding near his home. He had been shot, and police believe it was because he had either refused to join the cult, or else told them he was leaving. Canon Dominic Walker, the Church of England expert on the occult, says that in Satanism the rules of retribution for offenders are severe.

Police Chief Davidson also said that there had been reports of grave desecration and other necromantic pursuits in the area, but that the sacrificial killing was the first instance any parents in the town had known their children were involved in Satanic cults.

Amongst Satanic regalia found in many of the students' rooms and lockers which the police searched were such things as black robes, black candles, sacrificial knives and inverted cross medallions.

Law of the Inverted Cross

The reversal of Christianity is Satan's Law. It is a law unto itself and a religion to which the Friends of Hecate are dedicated in their apparent determination to break down British society as it exists today and, indeed, to bring about the destruction of all Christian values – and of those holding them – in the broadest interpretation of its meaning. Whilst they are not a political group as such, their allegiance being first and foremost to the black mass, they will of course use politics, particularly fringe groups and extremists, in furtherance of their aims. In this way their nefarious activities impinge upon every aspect of our society.

It seems likely that they are being assisted – unwittingly, perhaps – by developments in modern technology, in particular by the appropriation and distribution of real video 'nasties' which whet the appetite for bloodlust and help provide Satanic and allied groups with the mindless thugs they require at the bottom end of their organisations for action when the time is ripe.

The general apathy which seems to exist everywhere today is another fertile source of the seeds of discontent, and here again frustrated young people are the ones mostly at risk. Each year, for example, many of them come to London in search of success or to realise their potential and fulfil their dreams. Some find what they are looking for: most do not. And whilst the streetwise ones survive for a time, others tend to end up fraught with disillusion and slip into the sleazy social twilight zone which seems to be a compulsory part of every large city.

In time these young people just literally disappear. Over 600 annually in London alone are never heard of again. What happens to them? Are they merely victims – in their naivety – of the lure of the big city or are there more sinister reasons for their disappearance? How many of them fall into the hands of the Satanic cults?

In this respect, Paul Sturgess, General Secretary of the Christian Exorcism Study Group, says that some Satanic groups will sacrifice a human being if they possibly can; often these victims are unwanted babies or tramps taken from the streets at night. He also describes a typical initiation ceremony at which the initiate would firstly be drugged, either by injection or orally, and a doctor or nurse would take a blood sample from them. This sample is mixed with the blood of a sacrificed animal and drained into a chalice containing urine provided by the male priests of the Satanic 'temple' and the whole concoction drunk by the initiate as well as by the other members. The initiate is then made to undergo a bizarre stamina test to see how well he or she submits to the will of the group leader, and finally sexual intercourse takes place on a black altar. The initiate is totally unaware that the whole event is being secretly videoed, and it is this video tape which becomes the Satanic group's protection, the threat of its being shown to the initiate's family or employers ensuring his or her continued loyalty to the group.

Elymas, high priest of a white coven in Brighton, is more worried today than he has ever been about the general occult scene which he maintains is presently plagued by the increased use of drugs and by the large number of young people who are becoming interested in black magic and Satanism. In the Eastbourne and Battle areas of Sussex there are said to be several Satanist groups searching for suitable sites – especially places which have ley lines running through them – where they can practise in secret. He expresses the concern which he and other white witches feel now that so many old *Wiccan* sites are being used by those following the black arts which, by the very nature of their activities, harmfully affect the area thus precluding its future use by *Wicca*, and contaminating it generally.

In this connection he spoke of Clapham Wood which he and members of his coven visited on Candlemas this year (1986) and although they did not find any physical evidence of recent activity by the Friends of Hecate (thus confirming the belief of my colleagues and myself that they have temporarily vacated the site in favour of spreading into other areas), nevertheless Elymas said they were all extremely aware of the bad atmosphere prevailing within certain areas of the woods which he advised should be avoided at all costs. He said that none of the covens he knew would ever attempt to use such places because the forces there were so strong and the malignant atmosphere could cause mental and physical harm.

This, of course, is not surprising in view of the fact that devil worship has been going on in the Rape of Bramber generally, and Clapham Wood particularly, for the past one thousand years, which, even taking into account the probability that it was intermittent, would still mean a sizeable build-up.

It will be remembered that the initiate spoke of people in high places holding positions of power who would brook no interference, and over the past few years we have seen evidence of this alarming contributory factor to the breakdown of society by an increasing amount of corruption and scandal stemming from the highest institutions in the land, which is obviously calculated to undermine people's confidence in those who govern.

This view is strongly supported by Paul Sturgess, who comments that Satanists seek to achieve political and financial power and will go to extraordinary lengths to achieve this end. 'It is of great concern that Satanists can be found at the highest levels in our society in political life and on the boards of multi-national companies,' he says.

Mr Sturgess and others who monitor Satanic activities are convinced that some of the big Satanic groups are involved with international drug trafficking and blackmail. They believe that in Britain, Europe and the US there are Satanic cults practising with such a seriousness of purpose that they present a terrible danger to the general public and can indeed have a catastrophic effect upon the minds of those who are unprepared to combat them. All the evidence is there, and the findings of the Christian

154

researchers – once dismissed as cranks – are now being taken very seriously indeed.

So how can we combat this threat? Indeed, is there any way at all in which ordinary people can fight this psychic cancer? If so, what is the answer?

First of all we must all acknowledge that the threat exists. Just because we have not seen it happening before our own eyes, does not mean it is not there. All the evidence is there. Though the enemy amongst us is faceless, the battlefield non-geographical and hidden in the realms of the occult, and the weaponry disturbingly unconventional and of a psychic nature, nevertheless the effect on humanity of the unseen forces will be devastatingly real.

The next step after being made aware of the danger and recognising the nature of the threat, lies in our strength of mind.

In about 500 BC, a Chinese philosopher by the name of Lao Tsu said:

'Fighting is the most primitive way of making war on your enemies. The supreme excellence is to subdue their armies without having to fight them.'

Two thousand five hundred years further on, the war of the minds has arrived. It will involve every man, woman and child, and it will only be won by spiritual ascendancy. Only by this means will the advancing dark legions of the Inverted Cross be subdued: this is Lao Tsu's 'supreme excellence'.

BIBLIOGRAPHY

This book has grown out of Charles Walker's personal experiences, our original research, local Press reports, my own published articles and material from Alan Brown's unpublished manuscripts. Although great care has been taken in compiling this bibliography, if mention of any particular source has unfortunately been omitted, I can only tender my sincere apologies to those concerned.

ASHE, Geoffrey, *The Ancient Wisdom*, Macmillan Publishers (1976)

BAROJA, Julio Caro, *World of Witches*, Weidenfeld & Nicholson (1968)

BLUNSDON, Norman, *A Popular Dictionary of Spiritualism*, Arco (1962)

DEVEREUX, Paul, *The Ley Hunter's Companion*, Thames & Hudson (1972), *Earth Lights*, Thorsons Publishers (1982)

FORTUNE, Dion, *Psychic Self-Defence*, Aquarian Press, (c 1950)

FREEMANTLE, Brian, *KGB*, Michael Joseph Limited (1982)

GREEN, John Richard, *England Under Foreign Kings, A Short History of the English People*, Macmillan Publishers (1889)

HITCHING, Francis, *Earth Magic*, Picador (1976)

KING, Francis, *Sexuality, Magic and Perversion*, Spearman (Neville) (1972), *Satan and the Swastika* (1976)

LYTTON, Lord Bulwer, *A Strange Story* (1861), *The Coming Race*, Routledge & Kegan Paul (1871)

MACLELLAN, Alec, *The Lost World of Agharti*, Souvenir Press (1982)

MICHELL, John, *The New View Over Atlantis*, Thames & Hudson (1983)

MOORE and BERLITZ, *The Philadelphia Experiment: Project Invisibility*, Souvenir Press (1979)

MURRAY, Dr Margaret, *The Gods of Witches*, Oxford University Press (1970)

PAUWELS and BERGIER, *The Morning of the Magicians* (1960)

PINSENT, John, *Greek Mythology*, Hamlyn Publishing Group (1982)

RAVENSCROFT, Trevor, *Spear of Destiny*, Spearman (1972)

RUSSELL, Jeffrey B., *A History of Witchcraft, Sorcerers, Heretics and Pagans*, Thames & Hudson (1980)

SCHROEDER and OSTRANDER, *Psychic Discoveries Behind the Iron Curtain*, Sphere Books (1970)

TOMLINSON, John, *Left-Right: the March of Political Extremism in Britain*, Calder, John (Publishers) (1981)

UNDERWOOD, Guy, *The Pattern of the Past*, Pitman Publishing (1972)

VALIENTE, Doreen, *Where Witchcraft Lives*, Aquarian Press (1962)

WATKINS, Alfred, *Early British Trackways* (1922), *The Old Straight Track*, Sphere Books (1925)

WATSON, Dr Lyall, *Supernature*, Hodder & Stoughton (1973)

The Encyclopedia of Witchcraft and Demonology, Octopus Books (1974)

The New Larousse Encyclopedia of Mythology, Hamlyn Publishing Group (1968)

The Miracle of Man, Odhams Books (1943)

The Victoria History of the Counties of England; A History of the County of Sussex, ed. HUDSON, T.P., Vol. VI, Part I, Bramber Rape, Oxford University Press (1980)

INDEX

Entries followed by † can be found illustrated in the photo section between pages 96 and 97.